W9-ATO-191

Divorce and Remarriage: The Trojan Horse Within the Church

Whom Shall We Then Believe?

By
Joseph A. Webb Th.D., Ph.D.
&
Patricia L. Webb Ph.D.

*Divorce and Remarriage: The Trojan Horse
Within the Church
Whom Shall We Then Believe?*
by Joseph A. Webb Th.D., Ph.D. &
Patricia L. Webb Ph.D.

Printed in the United States of America

ISBN 978-1-60477-330-9

Christian Principles Restored Ministries
International, Inc.
P.O. Box 520729
Longwood, FL 32752-0729
Info @ cpr-ministries.org
www.cpr-ministries.org

www.xulonpress.com

Divorce and Remarriage: The Trojan Horse Within the Church

Whom Shall We Then Believe?

By
Joseph A. Webb Th.D., Ph.D.
&
Patricia L. Webb Ph.D.

Preface

In the February 2001 issue of Charisma Magazine Jack Hayford, gifted pastor, teacher and speaker, posed the question: "Do marriage vows matter?" He went on to say it is a question that sorely needs confronting in the church today. He said "it is confrontation needed to face down a mindset that, if left unchanged, will bring an onslaught of hellish delusions."

Linda S. Mintle, Ph.D. referred to this statement by Jack Hayford in an article in the June 2001 issue of Charisma Magazine entitled; "When the Vow Breaks." She said, "It's time for Christians to rethink divorce. Has the church taken on a secular view? Too often, yes."

Dr. Mintle went on to say; "That blur between secular and Christian views begins in the mind and heart. When we entertain the lies of our culture, we become disillusioned. Lies built on lies. They work on our feelings and eventually alter our relationships.

Over time we 'fall out of love' and excuse those who do the same."

According to Dr. Mintle, the consequences of such thinking are: "Divorce becomes the solution to unhappiness or lost passion. Marriage is no longer seen as a covenant but as a breakable contract. Happiness is the ultimate end."

Her solution was clear and simple: "We have entered into a holy covenant, before God; with another person: Good spouse, Bad spouse. Our mind-set should be 'till death do us part,' not 'till I'm unhappy.'"

The purpose of this book is to expose, in a non-judgmental way, where the Church is today in dealing with the divorce and remarriage issue. It will also explain how we arrived at this juncture and give a clear distinction regarding the secular and Christian worldviews on this vital subject. The bottom line will be; whom shall we then believe?

The answer to this question will determine where the church will find itself and what influence it will have in shaping society in a godly, biblical way in the decades to come.

"How be it when he, the Spirit of truth, is come he will guide you into all truth: for he shall not speak of himself, but whatsoever he shall hear, that shall he speak: and he will show you things to come. He shall glorify me: for he shall receive of mine, and shall show it unto you. All things that the Father hath are mine: therefore said I, that he shall take of mine, and shall show it unto you..." John 16:13-15
May God bless you as you study.

Acknowledgements
❧❧

The time-consuming work of writing and rewriting a book can only be appreciated by those who have experienced it themselves. Those few know well the value of having competent help in a project like this.

Rev. Clarence Lane, our son, was the first person to challenge us to rewrite <u>The Trojan Horse;</u> an eighteen page booklet.

Mrs. Cindy Wilson, Charles Lane and Jessica Lane came to our rescue with computer expertise and patience to see this task to its completion.

Additional extensive help was given by two dear fellow workers and friends, Dr. Edward Ware and his wife, Bonnie, of Aquila and Priscilla Ministries, Deland, Florida. Their unique ministry is one of encouraging pastors.

A former college classmate and retired businessman, Dan Bolhouse has been a continuous support in editing and encouragements. We thank God for the committed talents of these dear friends.

Joseph A. Webb and Patricia L. Webb

Table of Contents
❧❧

Introduction
ἐᴥἐᴥ

The Trojan Horse is a legend of the ancient Greeks, which some believe occurred in the 12th or 13th century, and is used today as a simile when describing someone who attempts to defeat another by deceit.

According to the legend, the Grecian states attacked the city of Troy, which is believed to have been in Asia Minor, present day Turkey; to rescue Helen, the wife of Sparta's king. As legend has it, Helen had been kidnapped by Paris, the son of Troy's king.

After 10 years of fighting outside the walls of Troy with no success, the Greeks devised a way to gain entrance to the city through trickery. To deceive the Trojans, they built a large, wooden horse on wheels and left it as a gift for the city of Troy. Then the Greeks sailed away.

The Trojans foolishly believed the battle was over and gleefully took the horse inside the city as a trophy; for horses were sacred animals to the Trojans.

As the Trojans were celebrating their victory, the Greek ships quietly returned, and Greek soldiers, hidden inside the hollow horse, crept out and opened the city gates for the invading army.

That night, the Greeks rescued Helen, killed the Trojans, desecrated their temples and burned Troy. Their victory was due to this one deceptive gift; the Trojan Horse.

Today, we see another Trojan Horse having a similar deceitful and devastating effect. This one however, is within the walls of what we call "the Church."

Church members are being warned about atheistic, evolutionary, amoral, humanistic, rationalism threatening our way of life. Since the leaders feel this threat is coming from outside the church, religious fellowships and denominations are organizing to resist and expose this philosophy. This counter assault by Christian leaders has increased at an unprecedented rate in their determination to stop this godless teaching from corrupting our Christian homes. We should all heartily concur and encourage these efforts being put forth.

Sadly however, while religious leaders are frantically pointing at the danger of rationalistic humanism outside the Church, many of these very same leaders are unknowingly, and we want to emphasize, unknowingly, teaching from their pulpits one of the most permissive and destructive concepts of humanistic doctrine ever devised by man: the present-day teachings concerning marriage, divorce and remarriage. As a result, the divorce rate in the Church is higher today than in the unchurched world. Pastors are now divorcing and remarrying at an unprecedented rate. Prudence therefore requires us to re-evaluate how the Church has arrived at its present doctrinal position on this subject. Where did our present day teaching begin?

We present these facts to you now and pray that you will honestly study to see if this teaching is true. The only request we make is for you to keep an open mind and evaluate everything, to make sure it is consistent with Scripture and Church history.

Francis Schaeffer wrote a book in 1976 entitled, *How Shall We Then Live?* Schaeffer laid out two worldviews, the secular and the biblical, and compared them with each other; declaring we must all decide how we are to live in the light of these two worldviews.

As you read this book, you will be faced with a similar dilemma. You will be confronted with a humanistic worldview and a biblical worldview concerning divorce and remarriage. As you read you will soon find a new question arises: That question will be, Whom shall we then believe?

"With each new evidence of deterioration, we lament for a moment, and then become accustomed to it!"

"...As behavior worsens, the community adjusts its standards to that conduct once thought reprehensible but is no longer deemed so."

Robert Bork
Slouching to Gomorrah

Chapter 1

Teachings of the Early Church on Marriage, Divorce and Remarriage
ই৯ই৯

What sources have been influencing our present conviction about divorce and remarriage? How did the earliest Church fathers interpret the pertinent passages in comparison to present day teachings? A fresh look back to the origins might be very insightful and helpful for those who truly desire to be faithful men and women of the Word.

Paul's challenge to Timothy reads:

Thou therefore, my son, be strong in the grace that is in Christ Jesus. And the things that thou hast heard of me among many witnesses, the same <u>commit thou to faithful men, who shall be able to teach others also.</u> II Timothy 2:1-2

1

Paul spent several years in the Arabian Desert, and while there, he received an all encompassing divine revelation directly from Jesus Christ:

But I certify you, brethren, that the gospel which was preached of me is not after man. For I neither received it of man, neither was I taught it, but by the revelation of Jesus Christ. Galatians 1:11,12

When speaking to the Corinthian church concerning the putting away of a marriage partner, Paul attributed his position as coming by divine revelation, directly from Jesus Christ.

And unto the married I command, yet not I, but the Lord, Let not the wife depart from her husband: But and if she depart, let her remain unmarried, or be reconciled to her husband: and let not the husband put away his wife. I Corinthians 7:10, 11

The earliest Church fathers are the *"faithful men"* Paul spoke about; many of whom were faithful unto martyrdom. They carried the purest truth available directly from *"other faithful men,"* *so* their teachings should give us a clear idea of what they believed Jesus and Paul taught on this subject.

As New Testament Christians and New Testament Churches, we should be desirous of conveying the heart of God above all else, and know what we teach is based on Scripture having come through *"faithfull men"* who perpetuated the teaching of Jesus and Paul. Any presumptive departure from those sources will be akin to building a house upon the sand. Therefore, it is vital we be aware of the seriousness of the Apostle Paul's teachings concerning marriage.

Such a teaching should cause us to look again to ensure what the Church teaches today, is what Jesus Christ and Paul taught.

The following material contains direct quotations of the earliest Church Father's teachings on marriage and divorce, and is edited from www. marriagedivorce.com, a website of Theological Foundations Ministries.[i]

The Church Fathers who were in positions of responsible authority, called and appointed by God to serve His Church, were required as shepherds of His sheep, to walk as He walked, and to talk as He talked. Their words are good counsel, and should be weighted most heavily in today's court of Christian opinion.

Nevertheless, the Church Fathers' teachings should in no wise be considered infallible or without possible error. Like us, they were privileged to be standard bearers and light holders for the God of the Universe in their generations, and like us, were faulty sinners saved by Grace. Those first Christians were close to ground zero...the very epicenter of the Christian earthquake that shook the world. This proximity in time and place to the ministry of Jesus Christ and His personally appointed Apostles gave them a much clearer vantage point than we enjoy today. We can look back through their writings to evaluate their legacy, by the lives they lived and the fruit of their labors.

These men of God had the initial responsibility of accurately defining and defending what the teachings and redemption Gospel of Jesus Christ meant. This responsibility was not only to the millions of lost souls in their world, but to the billions of lost souls in ours as well. Their theology was rooted in Christ; their lives were poured out in their present and their minds looked toward the future.

The early church fathers were in complete agreement. Of all the early recognized Church Fathers who ever wrote or who were written about concerning every discussion and every debate in thousands of surviving documents over hundreds of years, there is not a single dissenting authoritative voice on the essential core doctrines of marriage, divorce and remarriage. Each taught the same doctrine, each held the same opinion and each enforced the same moral standards as you will read here.

Hermas (A.D. 90)

Hermas was sold into slavery and sent to Rome as a boy. He was later set free by his owner, a woman called Rhoda. He became known as one of the authoritative Fathers of the Church and an influential Christian writer, noted for his detailed description of early Christianity. His surviving book, *The Shepherd*, was considered an inspired book of the Holy Bible until the fourth century A.D. To quote the translators: "The Shepherd of Hermas is in form, an apocalypse.

It consists of a series of revelations made to Hermas by the church, who appears in the form of a woman, by the shepherd, the angel of repentance, and by the great angel who is in charge of Christians. Each revelation is accompanied by an explanation and from these it can be seen, though the form of the book is apocalyptic and visionary, its object is practical and ethical."

Hermas wrote:

> The husband should put her away, and remain by himself. But if he put his wife away and marry another, he also commits adultery.

"I charge you" said he "to guard your chastity, and let no thought enter your heart of another man's wife, or of fornication, or of similar iniquities; for by doing this you commit a great sin. But if you always remember your own wife, you will never sin. For if this thought enters your heart, then you will sin; and if, in like manner, you think other wicked thoughts, you commit sin. For this thought is great sin in a servant of God. But if any one commits this wicked deed, he works death for himself. Attend, therefore, and refrain from this thought; for where purity dwells, there iniquity ought not to enter the heart of a righteous man." I said to him, "Sir, permit me to ask you a few questions." "Say on," said he. And I said to him, "Sir, if any one has a wife who trusts in the Lord, and if he detect her in adultery, does the man sin if he continues to live with her?" And he said to me, "As long as her remains ignorant of her sin, the husband commits no sin, the husband commits no transgression in living with her. But if the husband know that his wife has gone astray, and if the woman does not repent, but persists in her fornication, and yet the husband continues to live with her, he also is guilty of her crime, and a sharer in her adultery. And I said to him, what then, sir is the husband to do, if the wife continue in her vicious practices?" And he said, "The husband should put her away, and remain by himself. But if he put his wife away and marry another, he also commits adultery." And I said to him, "What if the woman put away should repent, and wish to return to her husband: shall she not be taken back by her husband?"

And he said to me, "Assuredly. If the husband do not take her back, he sins, and brings a great sin upon himself; for he ought to take back the sinner who has repented...in this matter man and woman are to be treated exactly in the same way."
(The Shepherd 4:1-10) (a)
Hermas taught:

❖ If a wife persists in adulterous behavior the "innocent party" may, and should, divorce in order to separate away from the sins of the offender.

6

❖ If a husband divorces his wife for such a reason he must remain single and not remarry. If a wife repents of her offense the husband must forgive her and receive her back as wife.

❖ If the husband does not forgive his repentant wife he brings a great sin upon himself.

❖ Men and women are to act and be regarded exactly the same in this matter.

Authors Note:
- Is this what your church teaches?
- Is this what you teach and believe?
- This is what the New Testament Church taught.

Justin Martyr (A.D.151)

Justin Martyr was one of the great, early theologians and apologists for the Church. He had the distinction of presenting a defining explanation and defense of Christianity to Caesar and the Imperial Roman Senate. His *Apology for the Christians,* written to refute charges of sedition to the Roman state, is a magnificent legal testimony of the power of early Christians to live holy and pleasing lives in an evil, corrupt society. Justin was beheaded for refusing to sacrifice to pagan gods.

Justin Martyr wrote:

"In regards to chastity, Jesus has this to say:

'If anyone look with lust at a woman, he has already before God committed adultery in his heart.' And, 'Whoever marries a woman who has been divorced from another husband, commits adultery.' According to our teacher, just as they are sinners who contract a second marriage, even though it is in accord with human law, so also are they sinners who look with lustful desires at a woman. He repudiates not only one who actually commits adultery, but even one who wishes to do so; for not only our actions are manifest to God, but even our thoughts." (First Apology 15) (a)

Justin Martyr taught:
- ❖ To indulge in lust is to be guilty of adultery of the heart.
- ❖ Whoever marries a divorced person commits adultery.
- ❖ Whoever contracts a second marriage is sinning against God (while a former spouse lives).
- ❖ God does not, and the Church must not, take into account human law when it is in violation of God's law.

8

❖ God judges motives and intentions, private thought life and actions. All is known and exposed to the God with which we have to do.

Authors Note:
- Is this what your church teaches?
- Is this what you teach and believe?
- This is what the New Testament Church taught.

Clement of Alexandria (A.D.208)

Titus Flavius Clemens, known as Clement of Alexandria, was a Greek theologian who served as head of the famous Catechetical School in Alexandria. His writings were designed to guide mature Christians to a more perfect knowledge of God and a pure moral character. His defense of the faith exhorted morals, kindness and patience. He taught that the thoughts and will of God in the Scriptures exhorts, educates and perfects the true Christian. Many scholars believe he founded the great Alexandrian School of Theology. He is listed as a martyr for his faith.

Clement of
Alexandria wrote:

"That Scripture counsels marriage, however, and never allows any release from the union, is expressly contained in the law: 'You shall not divorce a wife, except for reason of adultery.' And it regards as adultery the marriage of a spouse, while the

> And it regards as adultery the marriage of a spouse, while the one from whom a separation was made is still alive.

one from whom a separation was made is still alive. 'Whoever takes a divorced woman as wife commits adultery,' it says; for 'if anyone divorce his wife, he debauches her;' that is, he compels her to commit adultery. And not only does he that divorces her become the cause of this, but also he that takes the woman and gives her the opportunity of sinning; for if he did not take her, she would return to her husband."

(Miscellanies 2:23:145:3) (a)

Clement of Alexandria taught:
- ❖ The Scriptures encourage Christians to enter a marriage relationship.
- ❖ The marriage union covenant is permanent and does not allow anyone to be released from the union.
- ❖ Adultery is the only legitimate reason for divorce, otherwise separation is prohibited. Remarriage while a former spouse is alive is living in the state of adultery and is expressly forbidden in Scripture.
- ❖ A man who divorces his wife violates and corrupts her, for if she remarries for any reason except for the death of her

husband, she becomes an adulteress.

❖ The person who marries a divorced spouse sins not only by committing adultery with another's spouse but also sins against God by acting as an impediment to reconciliation of the original marriage.

❖ If the divorced spouse had remained single she would have, if possible returned to the first union.

Authors Note:

- Is this what your church teaches?
- Is this what you teach and believe?
- This is what the New Testament Church taught.

<u>Origen</u> (A.D. 248)

Origen is known as the most accomplished and significant theologian of the early Church. As a student and to exegete of the Old New Testaments, he influenced the critical thinking of the Church in his day to

> Just as a woman is an adulteress, even though she seems to be married to a man, while a former husband yet lives, so also a man who seems to marry who has been divorced does not marry her, but, according to the declaration of our Savior, he commits adultery with her.

such an extent that his works continue to have a major impact on doctrine and practice. He was the first teacher known to use the "allegorical" method of scriptural interpretation. It is estimated that he wrote some 5,000 thesis, tracts, epistles and books in his lifetime of service. Much of his work concentrated on refuting dangerous error and heresy. Origen was imprisoned during the reign of Emperor Decius. He was tortured to such an extent that he died from his ordeal after being released.

Origen wrote:

"For confessedly he who puts away his wife when she is not a fornicator, makes her an adulteress, so far as it lies with him, for if, 'when the husband is living she shall be called an adulteress if she be joined to another man;' and when by putting her away, he gives to her the excuse of a second marriage, very plainly in this way he makes her an adulteress...just as a woman is an adulteress, even though she seems to be married to a man, while a former husband yet lives, so also the man who seems to marry who has been divorced does not marry her, but, according to the declaration of our Savior, he commits adultery with her."

(Commentaries on Matthew 14) (a)

Origen taught:

❖   A man that divorces his wife who is not guilty of fornication causes her to become an adulteress if she remarries, and the man that marries her is an adulterer.

❖ The marriage covenant between a man and a woman is permanent as long as both husband and wife are alive.

❖ No matter what the legal circumstances may appear to be, a remarriage relationship entered into when either or both parties are divorced and a former partner lives, is adultery. The intimate relations between the man and the woman remarried while former spouses still live are adulterous, and considered sin.

❖ A remarriage is not an actual marriage, but disguised adultery.

Authors Note:
- Is this what your church teaches?
- Is this what you teach and believe?
- This is what the New Testament Church taught.

Basil the Great (A.D. 375)

Basil was born in Caesarea and educated in Athens. He is considered one of the great Fathers and Doctors of the Church. His writings include, *On the Holy Spirit* and *Moralia.* He was asked by the Church to help defend against the Arian heretical doctrines and subsequently became Bishop of Caesarea in 370. Basil became "Basil the Great" because of his outstanding personal integrity and holiness as well as his brilliance as a theologian and defender of the faith.

Basil the Great wrote:

"The man who has deserted his wife and goes to another is himself an adulterer because he makes her commit adultery; and

> The woman who lives with an adulterer is an adulteress the whole time.

the woman who lives with him is an adulteress, because she has caused another woman's husband to come over to her...the woman who lives with an adulterer is an adulteress the whole time. The woman who has been abandoned by her husband, ought, in my judgment, to remain as she is. The Lord said, 'If any one leave his wife, saving for the cause of fornication, he causes her to commit adultery, thus by calling her adulteress.' He excludes her from intercourse with another man. For how can the man being guilty, as having caused adultery, and the woman, go without blame, when she is called an adulteress by the Lord for having intercourse with another man? A man who marries another man's wife who has been taken away from him will be charged with adultery." Amphilochius 199 (a)

Basil Taught:

❖ A man that deserts his wife and she remarries another, makes his wife commit adultery.

❖ The woman who a divorced man marries is guilty of adultery.

❖ The second woman is guilty of taking another woman's husband.

❖ An adulterous relationship is continuous adultery, not a one time sin.

❖ An abandoned wife is to remain as she is and not remarry.

❖ An abandoned woman that takes another man and has sexual intercourse with him is committing adultery.

❖ If a man is guilty of adultery, so is a woman.

❖ It is a serious offense for a woman to take another woman's husband; she will be charged with adultery.

❖ It is a serious offense for a man to take another man's wife; he will be charged with adultery.

Authors Note:

• Is this what your church teaches?
• Is this what you teach and believe?
• This is what the New Testament Church taught.

Ambrose of Milan (A.D. 387)

Ambrose is known as one of the four original Doctors of the Church. Born in Germany and educated in Rome, Ambrose was asked to be

Bishop of Milan because of his extraordinary kindness and wisdom, which earned him the love and esteem of his people. History records that he publicly confronted,

> As regards marriage, the law is not to marry again, nor to seek union with another wife.

rebuked, and led to repentance Caesar Theodosius over the slaughtering of thousands of Thessalonians. He wrote major treatises on Christian morality and personal holiness, warning against adopting the world's standards. He was by all accounts a most extra-ordinary man, equal to his times. He was influential in bringing Augustine into a saving personal knowledge of Jesus Christ and receiving him into the Body of Christ.

Ambrose of Milan wrote:

"But what shall I say about chastity, when only one and no second union is allowed? As regards marriage, the law is not to marry again, nor to seek union with another wife. It

> He (John the Baptist) knew well that he would die as He was against the king, but He preferred virtue to safety.

seems strange to many why impediment should be caused by a second marriage entered on before baptism, so as to prevent election to the clerical office, and to the reception of the gift of ordination; seeing that even crimes are not wont to stand in the way, if they have been put away in the sacrament of baptism. But we must learn that in baptism sin can be forgiven, but law cannot be abolished. In the case of marriage there is no sin, but there is a law. Whatever sin there is can be put away, whatever law there is cannot be laid aside in marriage."

(On the duties of Clergy: 1: 257) (a)

"And what else did John have in mind but what is virtuous, so that he could not endure a wicked union even in the king's case, saying: 'It is not lawful for thee to have her to wife.' He could have been silent, had he not thought it unseemly for himself not to speak the truth for fear of death, or to make the prophetic office yield to the king, or to indulge in flattery. He (John the Baptist) knew well that he would die as he was against the king, but he preferred virtue to safety. Yet what is more

expedient than the suffering which brought glory to the saint."

(On the duties of Clergy, 3:89) (a)

"No one is permitted to know a woman other than his wife. The marital right is given you for this reason: lest you fall in a snare and sin with a strange woman. 'If you are bound to a wife do not seek a divorce,' for you are not permitted, while your wife lives to marry another."

(Abraham 1:57:59) (a)

"You dismiss your wife, therefore, as if by right

and without being charged with wrongdoing; and you suppose it is proper for you to do so because no human law forbids it; but divine law forbids it. Anyone who obeys men should stand in awe of God. Hear the Word of the Lord, which even they who propose our laws must obey: 'What God has joined together, let no man put asunder.'"

(Commentary on Luke, Sec. 8:5) (a)

Ambrose of Milan taught:

- ❖ Sex is a marital right that is limited to one's own husband or wife. Legitimate sexual relations with one's spouse protects from sexual sin.
- ❖ Extramarital sex is sin and a snare that will catch and kill.
- ❖ It is forbidden by God for a spouse to divorce and to remarry another.
- ❖ Ambrose interprets Paul's writings in Corinthians to mean that it is forbidden for a man or woman to remarry another while a former or earlier spouse lives.
- ❖ It is a wrong understanding to believe that it is simply one's right to divorce a spouse. Even though human law may permit such a thing, God strictly forbids it.
- ❖ Anyone who follows human customs and laws regarding marriage, divorce and remarriage instead of Divine laws should stand in fearful awe of God.
- ❖ All lawmakers, both in and out of the

Church, are warned to their peril to hear and obey the Word of the Lord.

❖ Jesus' command is reaffirmed: "What God has joined together, let no man put asunder."

❖ Conversion to Christianity forgives past sin, but does not nullify or set aside God's laws.

Authors Note:

- Is this what your church teaches?
- Is this what you teach and believe?
- This is what the New Testament Church taught.

<u>Jerome</u> (A.D. 396)

Jerome was another great Father and Doctor of the early Church whose most important work was the translation of the Bible into Latin (The Vulgate). He wrote works defending the Church from Jovinian, Vigilantius and Pelagianism heretics that were threatening the Gospel of Jesus Christ.

Jerome wrote:

"In explaining the testimony of the apostle, 'The wife hath not power of her own body, but the husband; and likewise, also, the husband hath not power of his own body, but the wife,' we have subjoined the following: 'The entire question relates to those who are living in wedlock, whether it is

19

lawful for them to put away their wives, a thing which the Lord also has forbidden in the Gospel.'

Following the decision of the Lord the apostle teaches that a wife must not be put away saving for fornication, and that, if she has been put away, she cannot during the lifetime of her husband marry another man, or, at any rate, that she ought, if possible, to be reconciled to her husband. In another verse he speaks to the same effect: 'The wife is bound...as long as her husband liveth; but if her husband be dead, she is loosed from the law of her husband; she is at liberty to be married to whom she will; only in the Lord.

I find joined to your letter of inquiries a short paper containing the following words: 'ask him, (that is me,) whether a woman who has left her husband on the ground that he is an adulterer and sodomite and has found herself compelled to take another may in the lifetime of him whom she first left be in communion with the church without doing penance for her fault.' As I read the case put I recall the verse 'they make excuses for their sins.'

> We are all indulgent to our own faults; and what our own will leads us to do we attribute to a necessity of nature.

We are all indulgent to our own faults; and what our own will leads us to do we attribute to a necessity of nature. It is as though a young man were to say, 'I am over-borne by my body, the glow of nature kindles my passions, the structure of my

20

frame and its reproductive organs call for sexual intercourse.' Or again a murderer might say, 'I was in want, I stood in need of food, I had nothing to cover me. If I shed the blood of another, it was to save myself from dying of cold and hunger.'

Tell the sister, therefore, who thus enquires of me concerning her condition, not my sentence but that of the apostle. 'Know ye not, brethren (for I speak to them that know the law,) how that the law hath dominion over a man as long as he liveth? For the woman which hath an husband is bound by the law to her husband, so long as he liveth; but if the husband be dead, she is loosed from the law of her husband. So then, if, while her husband liveth, she be married to another man, she shall be called an adulteress.' And in another place: 'the wife is bound by the law as long as her husband liveth; but if her husband be dead, she is at liberty to be married to whom she will; only in the Lord.'"

Authors Note:

Isn't it interesting; Jerome didn't know that portion of scripture didn't apply to marriages as some say today? Later on we will see when this deception was created and propagated.

The apostle has thus cut away every plea and has clearly declared that, if a woman marries again while her husband is living, she is an adulteress.

"You must not speak to me of the violence of a ravisher, a mother's pleading, a father's bidding, the influence of relatives, the insolence and the intrigues of servants, household losses. A husband may be an adulterer or a sodomite, he may be stained with every crime and may have been left by his wife because of his sins; yet he is still her husband and, so long as he lives, she may not marry another.

The apostle does not promulgate this decree on his own authority but on that of Christ who speaks in him. For he has followed the words of Christ in the gospel: 'whosoever shall put away his wife, saving for the cause of fornication, causeth her to commit adultery: and whosoever shall marry her that is divorced, committeth adultery.' Mark what he says: 'whosoever shall marry her that is divorced committeth adultery.' Whether she has put away her husband or her husband her, the man who marries her is still an adulterer.

I have not been able quite to determine what it is that she means by the words 'has found herself compelled' to marry again. What is this compulsion of which she speaks? Was she overborne by a crowd and ravished against her will? If so, why has she not, thus victimized, subsequently put away her ravisher? Let her read the books of Moses and she will find that if violence is offered to a betrothed virgin in a city and she does not cry out, she is punished as an adulteress: but if she is forced in the field, she is innocent of sin and her ravisher alone is amenable to the laws. Therefore if your sister, who, as she says, has been forced into a second union, wishes to receive the body of Christ and not to be accounted an adulteress, let her do penance; so far

22

at least as from the time she begins to repent to have no farther intercourse with that second husband who ought to be called not a husband but an adulterer. If this seems hard to her and if she cannot leave one whom she has once loved and will not prefer the Lord to sensual pleasure, let her hear the declaration of the apostle: 'ye cannot drink the cup of the Lord and the cup of devils: ye cannot be partakers of the Lord's table and of the table of devils,' and in another place: 'what communion hath light with darkness? and what concord hath Christ with Belial?'"

(Letters 55, 58) (a)

Jerome taught:

❖ The Lord has forbidden divorce and remarriage in the gospel.

❖ Christians must stop making excuses and stop trying to find justification for divorce and remarriage. None of it stands before God, and must not be considered at all when applying the Word of God in the Church or to our individual lives.

❖ A marriage is for life, and no matter what a spouse turns out to be, or how they may act, or the sins they commit, the covenant remains fully in effect. God does not divide the one flesh relationship.

❖ A spouse that is separated or divorced for any reason, no matter how provoked or how circumstances came to be as they are, is still bound to the marriage covenant and cannot be remarried to another as long as both live.

Authors Note:
- Is this what your church teaches?
- Is this what you teach and believe?
- This is what the New Testament Church taught.

<u>Augustine</u> (A.D. 419)

Augustine is widely regarded to be the single greatest Church leader and theologian between the time of the Apostles of Jesus Christ and the Reformation...perhaps beyond. His personal testimony of seeking and finding God after an early life of sin is as fresh and new today and as transparently Spirit-filled as it was then. His place in the Church among his peers can be compared to what Paul's was among the Apostles. He rigorously and effectively defended the faith from enemies on all sides. His writings are credited with influencing to an enormous extent the thinking of the great leaders of the Reformation.

Augustine wrote:

"This we now say, that, according to this condition of being born and dying, which we know, and in which we have been created, the marriage of male and female is some good, the compact whereof

24

divine Scripture so commends, as that neither is it allowed one put away by her husband to marry, so long as her husband lives; nor is it allowed one put away by his wife to marry another, unless she who have separated from him be dead.

Our Lord, therefore, in order to confirm that principle, that a wife should not lightly be put away, made the single exception of fornication; but enjoins that all other annoyances, if any such should happen to spring up, be borne with fortitude for the sake of conjugal fidelity and for the sake of chastity; and he also calls that man an adulterer who should marry her that has been divorced by her husband. And the Apostle Paul shows the limit of this state of affairs, for he says it is to be observed as long as her husband liveth; but on the husband's death he gives permission to marry.

For he himself also held by this rule, and therein brings forward not his own advice, as in the case of some of his admonitions, but a command by the Lord when he says: 'And unto the married I command, yet not I, but the Lord, Let not the wife depart from her husband: but and if she depart, let her remain unmarried, or be reconciled to her husband: and let not the husband put away his wife.' I believe that, according to a similar rule, if he shall put her away, he is to remain unmarried, or be reconciled to his wife."

(Commentaries on the Sermon on the Mount, Harmony of the Gospels, Homilies on the Gospels) (a)

"For whosoever putteth away his wife except for the cause of fornication, maketh her to commit adultery. To such a degree is that marriage compact entered upon be a holy Sacrament, that it is not made void even by separation itself, since so long as her husband lives, even by whom she hath been left, she commits adultery in the case where she marries another, and he who hath left her is the cause of this evil. But I marvel, if it be allowed to put away a wife who is an adulteress, so it be allowed, having put her away, to marry another.

For holy Scripture makes a hard knot in this matter in that the apostle says, that, by commandment of the Lord, the wife ought not to depart from her husband, but, in case she shall have departed to remain unmarried, or to be reconciled to her husband...I can not see how the man can have permission to marry another, in the case where he left an adulteress, when a woman can not be married to another when she left an adulterer.

Seeing that the compact of marriage is not done away with by an intervening divorce, so that they continue as wedded persons one to another, even after separation, and commit adultery with those with whom they be joined, even after their own divorce, either the woman with the man, or the man with a woman.

Neither can it rightly be held that a husband who dismisses his wife because of fornication and marries another does not commit adultery. For there is also adultery on the part of those who, after the repudiation of their former wives because of fornication, marry others....

No one is so unreasonable to say that a man who marries a woman whose husband has dismissed her because of fornication is not an adulterer, while maintaining that a man who marries a woman dismissed without the ground of fornication is an adulterer. Both of these men are guilty of adultery."

(Adulterous Marriages 1:9:9) (a)

"A spouse, therefore, is lawfully dismissed for cause of adultery, but the laws of chastity remains. That is why a man is guilty of adultery if he marries a woman who has been dismissed even for this very reason of adultery."

(ibid., 2:4:4) (a)

"A woman begins to be the wife of no later husband unless she has ceased to be the wife of a former one. She will cease to be the wife of a former one, however, if that husband should die, not if he commit adultery."

(ibid, 2:4:3) (a)

"Therefore to serve two or more (men), so to pass over from a living husband into marriage with another, was neither lawful then (in the Old Testament), nor is it lawful now, nor will it ever be lawful. To apostatize from the One God, and to go into adulterous superstitions of another, is ever an evil."

(On the Holy Spirit; Doctrinal Treatises; Moral Treatises) (a)

Augustine taught:

❖   It cannot be rightly held by those wishing to believe so, that anyone who divorces their spouse for adultery and then marries another is in the will of God and avoids the sin of adultery.

❖   It is adultery to marry another if someone is divorced and then chooses a new husband or wife.

❖   Whether or not a spouse commits adultery or fornication does not matter insofar as remarriage is concerned. Whoever remarries while a divorced spouse lives is in the state and sin of adultery.

❖   When a spouse remarries according to the law of the land after a divorce, they are still married to the former spouse as long as that spouse lives. Therefore the sexual and intimate relationship they have with a new spouse is simply engaging in a forbidden relationship by sinning with a person to whom they are not married in the eyes of God and the Church. Chastity refers to sexual abstinence. To have sexual relations with a remarried spouse is to be living in sin in direct disobedience to God's Word.

❖   A spouse can if they must, divorce their husband or wife who is guilty of adultery, but must not have a relationship with another as long as the original partner lives, for they are still in a binding life-long covenant with them.

❖ It is forbidden for a man or woman, even if they themselves were never previously married, to marry or have sexual relations with a divorced person whose spouse is still alive. They would be guilty of having sexual relations with another person's spouse, which is the very definition of the sin of adultery.

❖ It never has been lawful, is not now lawful, and it never will be lawful to divorce and remarry. To say and do otherwise is to adopt the adulterous superstitions of a different God than the one to which we have to do.

Authors Note:
- Is this what your church teaches?
- Is this what you teach and believe?
- This is what the New Testament Church taught.

Summary of Early Church Doctrine on Marriage, Divorce and Remarriage (90 A.D. - 419 A.D.)

❖ If a spouse persists in adulterous behavior and there is no other alternative, the marriage relationship can be terminated by the innocent party. (Hermas, Clement, Jerome, Augustine)

- ❖ Spouses that are divorced for any reason must remain celibate and single as long as both spouses live. Remarriage is expressly prohibited. (Hermas, Justin Martyr, Clement, Origen, Basil, Ambrose, Jerome, Augustine)
- ❖ To indulge in lust with the mind is to be guilty of adultery of the heart. (Justin Martyr)
- ❖ Whoever marries a divorced person commits adultery. (Hermas, Justin Martyr, Clement, Origen, Basil, Ambrose, Jerome, Augustine)
- ❖ Whoever contracts a second marriage while a former spouse lives sins against God, whether a Christian or not. (Justin Martyr, Ambrose)
- ❖ God does not, and the Church must not, take into account human law when it is in violation of God's law. (Justin Martyr, Origen, Ambrose)
- ❖ God judges motives and intentions, private thought life and actions. (Justin Martyr)
- ❖ The marriage covenant between a man and a woman is permanent, as long as both husband and wife are alive. (Clement, Origen, Ambrose, Jerome, Augustine)
- ❖ It is a serious offense against God to take another person's spouse. (Basil)
- ❖ The Church must charge all persons who are in possession of another living person's former husband or wife with adultery.

(Basil)

❖ Sexual relations are a marital right that is limited to one's own husband or wife. (Hermas, Justin Martyr, Clement, Origen, Basil, Ambrose, Jerome, Augustine)

❖ Sexual relations with one's legitimate spouse protects from sexual sin. (Ambrose)

❖ Marriage and sexual relations with a remarried spouse while a former spouse lives is the sin of adultery. (Hermas, Justin Martyr, Clement, Origen, Basil, Ambrose, Jerome, Augustine)

❖ It is a serious mistake to believe that it is simply one's right to divorce a spouse and take another. Even though human law may permit such a thing, God strictly forbids it. He cannot, He will not honor it. (Clement, Origen, Ambrose, Jerome, Augustine)

❖ Anyone who follows human customs and laws instead of God's Divine instructions regarding marriage, divorce and remarriage should stand in fearful awe of God Himself. (Clement, Ambrose).

❖ All lawmakers in and out of the Church are warned to their peril, to hear and obey the Word of the Lord in regard to His commands on marriage and divorce.

> Christians must stop making excuses and stop trying to justify divorce and remarriage.

❖ Christians must stop making excuses and

stop trying to justify divorce and remarriage. There are no valid reasons acceptable to God. (Jerome, Augustine)

❖ Marriage is for life. No matter what a spouse turns out to be or how they may act, no matter what they do or don't do, or the sins they commit, the covenant remains fully in effect. A remarriage while a former spouse lives is not marriage at all, but sinful adultery. God does not divide the one flesh relationship except by physical death. (Hermas, Clement, Origen, Basil, Ambrose, Jerome, Augustine)

❖ Marriage is a lifelong covenant that will never be invalidated by God while both parties live. (Hermas, Justin Martyr, Clement, Origen, Basil, Ambrose, Augustine) It never has been lawful, is not now lawful, and never will be lawful to divorce and remarry. To say and do otherwise is to worship and adopt the adulterous superstitions of a different god than the one to which we have to do. (Augustine)[ii]

Authors Note:
- Is this what your church teaches?
- Is this what you teach and believe?
- This is what the New Testament Church taught.

If we are reasonable people, we would have to say the teachers of the first through the third centuries were more pure and uncompromised in their teaching since they were so close to the source of all our truth-the Lord Jesus and the Apostles Paul and John the Beloved. These Early Church Fathers were still part and parcel of the practice initiated by the Apostle Paul. Again we are reminded of Paul's instructions when writing to Timothy, *"And the things that thou hast heard of me among many witnesses, the same commit thou to faithful men, who shall be able to teach others also." (II Timothy 2:2)*

The teaching then was still pure and undefiled by denominational corruption or the developing traditions of men. The Church Fathers clearly understood pure truth: one man, one woman, for life.

The permanence of the marriage covenant was the unanimous teaching of the early Church and continued to remain basically unchanged for fifteen centuries. These quotations were not, as some would suggest, their own private opinions, but their deeply held convictions based upon their proper "dividing" of God's word.

Four Major Doctrinal Conclusions Established by the Early Church Fathers

From the accumulated teachings of these earliest Church fathers, the early Church came to some basic doctrinal positions. These positions were their summary of all they had been taught and had taught others in their century.

Historically, from the first to the sixteenth century, there were only four basic theological positions (conclusions) on marriage, divorce, and remarriage in the early Christian church. <u>Paul Steele and Charles Ryrie, in their book *Meant To Last*</u> (Victor Books) and <u>William A. Heth and Gordon J. Wenham,</u> in their book *Jesus and Divorce* (Thomas Nelson Publishers) describe these four positions in detail. Each position is listed here by name and includes a short explanation. The first four positions, being the earliest and thus the oldest, are:

The patristic view (Early Father's View)

This view declared: If one were to suffer the misfortune of divorce, remarriage to a second spouse was not permitted regardless of the cause.

The preteritive view (Augustinian View)

This view interpreted Jesus' remarks in Matthew 19 to be refusing to take "adultery" as a cause for separation, divorce, or nullity. Remarriage is always wrong following a valid marriage.

The betrothal view (Engagement View)

This view interprets the Matthew 19:9 passage as an exception clause, applying only to a Jewish betrothal period and previous to consummating the actual marriage. Thus the word "fornication" and not "adultery" is used.

The consanguinity view (Unlawful Marriage View)

This view said divorce would be allowed only in the case of a "forbidden (incestuous) marriage," such as when close relatives married. Apart from this particular circumstance, neither divorce nor remarriage to a second spouse would be permitted.

All four of these earliest Church views concluded that the Bible clearly teaches marriage is for life and to remarry while your first partner is still alive constitutes adultery.

Steele and Ryrie also said:

"Careful research through the hundreds of manuscripts written by Church leaders of the first five centuries has revealed, that with only one exception (Ambrosiaster[iii] fourth century Latin writer) the Church fathers were unanimous in their understanding that Christ and Paul taught if one were to suffer the misfortune of divorce, remarriage was not permitted, regardless of the cause."[iv]

These were the only doctrinal conclusions the Early Church knew and continued to know for over fifteen hundred years concerning the permanence of the marriage covenant.

This remained the standard view of the Early Church until the sixteenth century. For the first time in Church history a Roman Catholic, Greek and Latin scholar, Disiderius Erasmus, suggested a new, previously unheard of doctrinal position

35

concerning marriage and divorce. This new idea was adopted by many of the new Protestant Theologians who had just come out of what was later called the Dark Ages, and were attempting to adjust and declare their new religious freedom and environment.

Chapter 2

Exposing the Enemy in the Camp
❧

The humanistic author of deception:

Desiderius Erasmus Roterodamus
- October 27, 1466, born in
  Rotterdam, Holland
- 1478 orphaned and sent to church
  schools
- 1486 entered an Augustinian
  monastery
- 1492 took vows to become a Roman
  Catholic priest.
- 1506 received a doctor of divinity degree in
  Turin, Italy
- 1510 befriended by Henry VIII, taught
  Greek at Cambridge University in England

- 1516 made the first translation of the Greek New Testament into English
- 1519 wrote tract on matrimony
- 1521 left England
- July 12, 1536, died in Basel, Switzerland

The humanistic instrument of deception:

The fifth view, which was not introduced until the sixteenth century, was called **"The Erasmian view:"** This view was written more than eleven hundred years after the four authentic historic views and, consequently does not qualify to be called an earliest Church father's view. When adopted and elaborated on by the reformers it was eventually renamed "The Traditional Protestant View." Doesn't it seem ironic when we realize a rationalistic, humanistic re-interpretation of the marriage doctrine was created by a Roman Catholic teacher and priest, ended up being titled; "The Traditional Protestant View?"

Disiderius Erasmus (1467-1536), after whom this historic doctrinal view was named, was otherwise known as Erasmus of Rotterdam. In university libraries today, he is called "the prince of humanists." After his death, the early Roman church declared Erasmus a heretic and all of his writings were banned or burned .[v] Later, the Pope had every existing anathema declared over Erasmus' grave and his bones were dug up and scattered.

"Although Erasmus is often regarded as a precursor of the Reformation and his works were later listed in the Index of Forbidden Books by the Council of Trent, his war against ignorance and superstition was prompted by his convictions as a humanist rather than as a theologian. He was not a religious reformer, as were Martin Luther and French theologian John Calvin; nor was he inclined to participate in theological discussions. He was first and foremost a man of letters, and as a humanist, he was at the forefront of his age."[vi] Erasmus wrote his paper on marriage and divorce in 1519. His conclusions on the subject were greatly influenced by his humanistic paradigm and total disregard of the earlier Church positions.

J.C. Grayson said, "...Erasmus wished to explain the Scriptures, unconstrained and not squeezed into the harness of doctrinal decisions and tradition."[vii]

Erasmus introduced a new idea in his treatise by saying, "any marriage which is capable of being dissolved was never a marriage at all."[viii] Whenever we hear such teaching, it is important to again compare it with the clear concise teachings of our Lord Jesus Christ.

We say again, this conclusion is without merit. This false doctrine was invented by a humanistic philosopher who birthed this heretical position, based upon a **false premise.** The Christian community adopted his false premise even though his teaching is clearly contrary to the historically clear teaching of God's Word and all of the earliest Church fathers. The family, which is the bedrock unit of our society, is disintegrating at an alarming rate as a result of adopting this false doctrine.

Despite Jesus' clear, non-contradictive teaching, the vast majority of today's religious leaders follow Erasmus' teachings.

> The family, which is the bedrock unit of our society, is disintegrating at an alarming rate as a result of adopting this false doctrine.

The Erasmian position allows for remarriage where adultery or desertion is involved.

Erasmus, who never left the Roman Catholic Church, deceptively "laid the egg and the reformers hatched it."[ix] Erasmus placed this erroneous theory, which I have called the Trojan Horse, before the Protestant reformers. They enthusiastically received it, not realizing the enemies it contained. Hiding inside this Trojan Horse were the devastating enemies; rationalism, humanism, compromise, distorted ideas of men, and doctrines of demons. These enemies represent the secularized humanistic worldview in contrast to a Biblical world view and display a total disregard for what Jesus, Paul and the earliest Church Fathers taught concerning marriage.

The religious societal environment that birthed this new wave of freedom of thought, rationalistic humanism, was one of total intellectual and spiritual bondage. If the Church in Erasmus' day said the earth was flat and you disagreed by saying it was round, you could be burned at the stake. If the

Church said that baptism is by sprinkling and you said that baptism is by immersion, you and your fellow believers stood in danger of being drowned by soldiers at your next baptismal service. There was no room whatsoever for dissent.

Erasmus was a free thinker, and after becoming famous for his publication of a critical edition of the Greek New Testament in 1516 and a second edition used by the translators of the "Authorized King James Version of the Bible," he was emboldened to write more aggressively. The article, *Desiderius Erasmus Roterdamus,* found in *Wikipedia, the Free Encyclopedia* states; "In Switzerland he, (Erasmus), was especially exposed to criticism through his association with men who were more than suspected of extreme rationalistic doctrines." He not only broke away from the normal boundaries of the Church, but also went on to say, **"Reason** is the only one guide of life, the supreme arbiter of all questions, politics and religion included."[x]

Using this as his overriding paradigm in approaching answers to problems he observed in the society in which he lived, Erasmus said, "it should be looked into if there may not be other interpretations which are to be read in the gospels and the epistles."[xi]

With this paradigm he proceeded to re-interpret Matthew 5 & 19 and 1 Corinthians 7 in an unprecedented way, forsaking all the early Church had ever taught. He ignored and twisted what Jesus, Paul the Apostle and the early Church Fathers

41

taught, to promote his humanistic convictions. He called their statements and teachings, "monstrous." Monstrous? Would you or I ever make such a charge? Do we dare be in agreement with someone who "Reasoned" that way? It might benefit us here to pause and analyze the full meaning of this accusation Erasmus made against the teachings of our Lord Jesus, Paul the Apostle, and every one of the earliest church fathers. The Webster's Dictionary describes this word to mean: "shocking in its wrongness and absurdity."

Synonyms of this word; "Monstrous" are even more enlightening of Erasmus' view of scripture and the sanctity of marriage.

- <u>Outrageous:</u> "extremely offensive"; "exceeding one's power to bear or endure."
- <u>Heinous:</u> "hatefully bad; such flagrant conspicuousness that it excites hatred or horror."
  - <u>Atrocious:</u> "such badness that it excites condemnation."

With this mindset, Erasmus attacked the sacredness of God's Word and the marriage covenant.

To Erasmus, it seemed "<u>monstrous</u> that a couple should be compelled to stay together in the flesh when they no longer and perhaps never were united in the spirit...forcing a couple to stay together when they detest one another is dangerous. It may end in poison. Those whose marriage is already on the rocks should be granted a divorce and permitted to remarry. Paul's dictum that it is better to marry than to be tormented by passion is not inapplicable to persons once unhappily married and now separated..." "The Church must not be bound by the *past.*"[xii] Paul said we must be bound and limited to *"My gospel." Romans 2:16*

Today, we must understand that we are not bound by the past but always restricted by the Word of God alone, in order that we can be free to please and serve God.

In his reasonings, Erasmus also concluded: "...the case of a youth who may have been caught into a marriage through wine and drunkenness. In such instances there are often mutual quarrels, irremediable hatred, dread of poisoning and murder, anticipating nothing but evil. Neither can live continently and if they cleave to each other they perish twice, but if the marriage is dissolved and they are allowed to marry again, it is hoped that they both should be outside peril."[xiii]

Erasmus did not say these things in an intellectual vacuum, but realized perfectly well in all of this argumentation that he was going counter to all former Church doctrine as well as current practice. "Erasmus appealed to consensus only on theological points about which he was not deeply concerned. On a matter of ethics, like marriage, he was ready to contravene the consensus for the sake of humane legislation."[xiv] It is clear that Erasmus' primary concern was not what the Word of God said, but rather, that man's happiness is most important.

"He (Erasmus) is aware of the common opinion which opposed remarriage after divorce for adultery, but he also knows that it lies within the hearts of good men to change their opinions in order to deal with a good cause. His conviction, evident throughout his approach, is that enlightenment would usher in a new era and bring reform within the Church. Two basic propositions are laid down. It should be permissible to dissolve certain marriages, not fortuitously but for very serious reasons, by the ecclesiastical authorities or recognized judges, and to give the innocent party the freedom to marry again. These two views were considered revolutionary and heretical by the theologians of his day."[xv]

"Erasmus brings the reader face to face with the problems of the many thousands who are unhappily coupled together with the result that both parties thereby perish. They could be saved if they were divorced and able to marry someone else. If this were possible without doing injury to the Word of God, then it ought to delight all godly men. Furthermore, charity sometimes does what it legally is not able to do, and it is justified in doing so. Erasmus realizes that this proposition may be regarded as unheard of and absurd, as well as being unworthy of being called into discussion...Erasmus would **reason** that it is against nature that the innocent party in a divorce case should not be allowed to remarry."[xvi]

Please keep in mind that these false premises, which sound so reasonable in today's churches, were previously unheard of and totally contrary to New Testament and early Church theology. They were in total opposition to the clear teachings of Scripture, and ignited a firestorm of greater rationalizations, when the reformers adopted and added to this corrupt unscriptural premise.

Chapter 3

*The Reformers, Erasmus,
the Trojan Horse*
❧❧

The historical definition of humanism, as applied to Erasmus' day, was the pursuit of a classical education, which included study of the literature and languages of the classical world, Latin and Greek.

> Humanism's core conviction is that man's happiness is most important.

Humanism's core conviction is that man's happiness is most important. This conviction led Erasmus to reinterpret some Scriptures in an unprecedented way. For the first time "porniea," from Matthew, chapters 5 and 19, was interpreted as general moral uncleanness or adultery, and therefore constituted legal grounds for divorce. His position says when divorce is allowed, it automatically breaks the union between the two partners and, therefore, reasonably allows for remarriage to another partner. He then concluded (reasoned) that if these were legal grounds, then the innocent party should be free to remarry; otherwise, one could not say that it was a legal divorce. Through this teaching Erasmus presented his insidious Trojan horse to the Reformers. As they drew it in, they began inventing even more excuses for divorce.

When Luther and the other reformers left the Roman Church for what they perceived to be new light and a greater truth, they also, being grateful of Erasmus' gift to them of the Greek translation, quickly accepted Erasmus' teachings concerning marriage and divorce. This unwise choice resulted in their abandonment of clear theology for humanistic "reasoning" concerning any teachings on marriage, divorce and remarriage. Consequently, they were influenced by Erasmus' new theory of "reasonableness" which opened a doctrinal Pandora's Box, resulting in the inclusion of many other unscriptural and forbidden excuses for granting a divorce. The following are some of their conclusions:

Martin Luther (1483 -1546)

Was a German monk, theologian, and church reformer. A highly educated man, Luther enrolled in law school before entering the Augustinian monastery. He later taught theology at the University of Wittenberg.

Luther introduced new, unprecedented Grounds for Divorce:

- If a woman is married to an impotent man.
- Ignorance of a former contracted marriage.
- Desertion: 2-10 yrs. I Corinthians 7:15; *"innocent remarry."*

Desertion was now perceived as legal grounds for divorce with the deserted party free to remarry.

The only decision the reformers were in conflict over was the length of time needed to declare that one had been deserted. Their conflicting conclusions varied from two to ten years.

Wife's objection to render the conjugal duty. I Corinthians 7:3-5.

Failure of a wife to perform normal conjugal responsibilities.

This suddenly constituted grounds for divorce and remarriage, especially if she had been previously warned. The title given to this false teaching today is "reverse fornication."

Adultery; Luther, using only Matthew & I

Corinthians Texts: Said, *"the innocent party can remarry."*

Adultery is grounds for divorce with the innocent party free to remarry.

Luther and the other Reformers, influenced by Erasmus, <u>reasoned</u> if one partner committed adultery in the Old Testament, God commanded them to be stoned. Thus, in God's sight, the guilty party was dead and the innocent party could remarry.

Isn't it strange how these men bypassed Jesus' treatment of the woman caught in the act of adultery? Did He tell them to stone her, or tell her she was forgiven and to *"go and sin no more" John 8:3-11*? They also bypassed Paul's treatise in Corinthians where he writes;

> *"Be not deceived: neither fornicators, nor idolaters, nor adulterers...shall inherit the kingdom of God. And such <u>were</u> some of you..." I Corinthians 6: 9-11*

If these teachings were scripturally true then Paul would have to be speaking to people who were already stoned or dead. *"...but ye are washed, but ye are sanctified, but ye are justified in the name of the Lord Jesus, and by the Spirit of our God." v. 11b.* Strangely enough, there is no mention of these people being dead or stoned.

Eventually Martin Luther concluded that all divorce matters should be decided by civil judges and magistrates, and not by the Church.[xvii]

50

Decisions about divorce now became the responsibility of secular power.

Eventually Martin Luther concluded that all divorce matters should be decided by civil judges and magistrates, and not by the Church.

"The government has to demand obedience, and it has to decide what is a rightful marriage. In Luther's discussion of divorce and remarriage, it was noticed that remarriage was justified by the fact that the adulterer was the same as dead in the eyes of God and in his relationship to the innocent party. Luther even felt that the adulterer deserved capital punishment."[xviii]

John Milton (1608–1674)

By the seventeenth century, John Milton; 1608-1674, a Protestant Puritan and author of "Paradise Lost and Paradise Found," enlarged upon another of Luther's conclusions, impotence being grounds for divorce and remarriage; by declaring a new exception where he contended; "If divorce was permissible for impotence, then it was equally well justified for incompatibility of mind and temperament."[xix] This reasoning process represented man's thinking and logic of that century. Here is a clear example of how our present day teaching evolved; one false conclusion was used to affirm another false conclusion.

Many pastors today have adopted this "reasoning" and are using it to justify divorce in their marriage, divorce, and remarriage counseling. This unscriptural premise, introduced by a man who had a negative experience in his marriage, has become one of the main pillars for "no fault" divorces.

Phillip Melanchthon (1497-1560)

Reformer, Phillip Melanchthon, a German professor, theologian and associate of Martin Luther, added these following reasons to the list of legitimate grounds for divorce and remarriage. He said, "The marriage tie is severed by the adulterer himself, and not by the innocent party, who is free. Therefore, when the judge declares the innocent party free, he should expressly state that he or she may enter another marriage with a clear conscience. When that declaration is made, the innocent party can marry at any time." Melanchthon does not, as does Luther, give any exegetical reasons why the innocent party may marry again. He only lays down the proposition: "if the innocent party was not allowed to marry again, it would be a divorce only in name and not in reality."[xx]

Huldreich Zwingli (1484-1531)

Zwingli was the leader of the Protestant Reformation in Switzerland and another humanist scholar.

"When Christ granted divorce on account of adultery, He did not exclude other reasons for divorce or prescribe this only but mentions this as one among many...it did not mean that adultery was the sole reason for divorce. There are other evils, which are even worse than adultery, as for example, treachery, sorcery, and parricide (murder). Only the secular authorities could make a divorce valid since they alone could make the marriage legal...therefore God marries, when the contracting parties are joined together in accordance with the ordinance and will of God, and the rites of the nation and the civil code. Hence they follow human, not divine tradition who say that mutual agreement is the only thing necessary for marriage. The magistrate is the minister of God. Hence those who abide by those laws, God marries them. Those who go against those laws, or whatever those laws condemn, God does not sanction their marriage."[xxi]

Martin Bucer (1491-1551)
-Quote by De Regno Christi in 1557

"The narratives of the Evangelist should be taken together when they are treating the same subject or incident, and the <u>briefer</u> <u>narratives</u> <u>of</u> <u>other</u> <u>Gospels</u> <u>should</u> <u>be</u> <u>harmonized</u> <u>with</u> <u>the</u> <u>fuller</u> <u>accounts</u> and interpreted with reference to other passages of Scripture relating to the same matter...thus, when the Lord in two places in Matthew most clearly allowed a concession about divorce, namely, in the case of adultery, then the same should be added to the words and replies of the Lord as recorded in Mark and Luke."[xxii]

These previously rejected reasonings now permitted couples to divorce and remarry with

Protestant Church approval.

This view, called the Matthew/Pauline Exception Theory is taught dogmatically and exclusively by nearly all churches today. These same teachings ignore the fact that Matthew was written to the Jews to prove Jesus was the promised Messiah. In Matthew Christ was addressing the Jewish tradition called "betrothal." This tradition is illustrated between Joseph and Mary. Joseph thought Mary had committed fornication and was going to divorce her quietly. In Matthew, and only in Matthew, Jesus used this word carefully to show it was still legal for a Jewish man or woman to get divorced "legally" from a betrothal, "not a marriage." To divorce and remarry after becoming married constituted adultery so long as your first partner lived. Christ did not give permission for a husband and wife to divorce and remarry, but applied that phrase; "except for fornication" to apply only to a betrothed couple.

We only need to observe what is happening to our families to see the kind of fruit Erasmus' teaching is producing. Jesus taught us, any tree with bad roots can only produce bad fruit. By following this teaching from Erasmus, thinking it is scripturally, and historically authoritative, millions of believers are having their families destroyed and suffering the terrible pain and agony of divorce and broken homes, with shattered family relationships, while being told by church leaders, "It is God's will, get on with your life."

The answer to our present day social disintegration is not divorce and remarriage, but a renewed emphasis of the necessity of all believers to manifest Christ likeness and deep humility, considering others better than ourselves, when facing marital difficulties. Paul said, in Romans 12:10; *"Be kindly affectioned one to another with brotherly love; in honour preferring one another."*

I pray that after researching this historic information for yourself, the Spirit of God will help you see the urgency of restoring biblical truth to the Church concerning marriage and divorce before it is eternally too late. Together we must pray the Church awakens to this erroneous, corrupt teaching destroying our marriages. *"My people are destroyed for lack of knowledge: because thou hast rejected knowledge."* Hosea 4:6. The Church must return to uncompromising New Testament truth for the healing of our nation's homes.

Whom will you and I believe? Will we believe Erasmus, who is historically described by his peers as a humanistic heretic? Will we believe his teachings on marriage and divorce despite their obvious contradiction of all the teachings of the earliest Christian fathers? Will we believe Erasmus when his teaching flies in the face of what Jesus Christ and Paul clearly taught?

In reviewing what we have learned, we must historically and doctrinally recognize the Erasmian view as false teaching, introduced by a man accused by his peers of having a distorted paradigm, with no sound exegetical foundation from Scripture; a man who totally ignored what every early Church Father before him taught on this subject, and who declared Jesus' and Paul's teachings about marriage, divorce, and remarriage to be "Monstrous!" His only solution went on to declare, "We need to reinterpret scripture and not depend on the past."[xxiii] Until we recognize this as a fallout, we will not be ready to go back to the Word of God, which is the only eternal authoritative source of all truth and is consistent with all the earliest Church Fathers' teachings on this subject.

The Erasmian view, and all of the spurious arguments that have been added to it by the Reformers, have produced the corrupted teachings presently polluting our churches with the vilest form of family-destroying, immoral humanism possible! The Apostle Paul warned believers against such teachings in Timothy, *"Now the Spirit speaketh expressly that in the latter times some shall depart from the faith, giving heed to seducing spirits and doctrines of devils." I Timothy 4:1*

Remember, any doctrine built upon a false premise is a false doctrine that will cause anyone who receives it to move from a scriptural answer to his or her "own misguided ideas." Here, Paul, under the inspiration of the Holy Spirit, gave each of us our marching orders:

> Any doctrine built upon a false premise is a false doctrine.

Preach the Word, be instant in season, out of season, reprove, rebuke, exhort with all long-suffering and doctrine for the time will come when they will not endure sound doctrine but after their own lusts shall they heap to them-selves teachers, having itching ears; and they shall turn away their ears from the truth....
II Timothy 4:2-4a, TLB

Erasmus and the reformers taught all Scripture verses about marriage and divorce must be interpreted in the light of Matthew, chapters 5 & 19. Proper hermeneutic rules for interpreting Scripture however, declare the opposite.

We cannot disregard the necessity for comparing Scripture with Scripture, while always remembering that the plain verses are the main verses. "All obscure and seemingly contradictory verses must submit to those portions which are clear and concise. In most instances the unclear will be cleared up by the clear, and a sound verdict can be rendered."[xxiv]

> What we believe means nothing unless all of Scripture agrees.

What we believe means nothing unless all of Scripture agrees.

All the verses which seem to contradict the concise verses come into total agreement when interpreted in a true hermeneutic progression.

Neither the Ten Commandments nor the teachings of Jesus were spoken by a God of judgment and anger. They came from the heart of a loving Heavenly Father who gave them so we may experience an abundant life of constant provision and blessing:

> *And he shall be like a tree planted by the rivers of water, that bringeth forth his fruit in his season; his leaf also shall not wither; and whatsoever he doeth shall prosper.*
> *Psalms 1:3*

This same God accompanied His laws and commandments with a sacrificial system that provided forgiveness,

> His desire is to let us know His way is perfect and all other ways lead to self-destruction.

reconciliation and renewed blessings to anyone who was willing to confess their sins to God and allow the Holy Spirit to lovingly lead them out of their life of disobedience. God's heart and attitude toward mankind has never been to judge or destroy. His desire is to let us know His way is perfect and all other ways lead to self destruction.

God did not demand the permanence of the marriage covenant to injure or torment us. Instead, His heart of love and mercy required its permanence to avoid the horrible destruction that disobedience to His standards brings. Today, much of our society and a growing number of churches have chosen to abandon God's clear commandments to accommodate man's selfish desires. The accompanying destruction from this abandonment is now being declared not only by the Church, but by an alarmed secular society as well. God's loving heart wants all of mankind to enjoy Him and life itself because His knowledge is perfect, complete, and founded in pure love. God gave us His inerrant Word as the only sure way to abundant life. It is neither God's goal nor His desire to punish or separate Himself from us. Rather, God's goal and desire is to bless us and make us to be a blessing; both light and salt, to this generation.

Jesus lovingly warned in Matthew:

Ye are the salt of the earth: but if the salt have lost his savour, wherewith shall it be salted? it is thenceforth good for nothing, but to be cast out, and to be trodden under foot of men. Matthew 5:13

Could it be that we are almost there as a Church? Are we changing the world with God's loving message of purity, or has the world changed us? The following statistics may provide a clue.

> It is neither God's goal nor His desire to punish or separate Himself from us.

Chapter 4

The Devastation of Divorce and Remarriage
✎✎

What is the fruit of this non-Biblical teaching on divorce? Our Lord Jesus declared, *"By their fruit you will know them."* *Matthew 7:20* If you would like to know the nature of the spring from which this teaching comes, just look at the fruit. The following research may serve to show the negative

> The greatest tragedy however, is the present day Church has now surpassed the unchurched world in the percentage of divorces and remarriages.

unchristlike effect of this Erasmian doctrine. These examples are not taken from religious of the sources, but from secular society's alarming statistics, and represent only a very small percentage available data. These statistics overwhelmingly validate the destruction caused by divorce and remarriage. The greatest tragedy however, is the present day Church has now surpassed the unchurched world in the percentage of divorces and remarriages. Consider the following:

Divorce is pervading our society. Twenty-five percent of adults aged 18-35 have lived through their parents getting divorced.
Elizabeth Marquardt *Between Two Worlds: The Inner Lives of Children of Divorce* (New York: Crown Publishers, 2005)

"Half of all children will witness the breakup of a parent's marriage. Of these, close to half will also see the breakup of a parent's second marriage."
Furstenberg, Peterson, Nord, and Zill, "Life Course," 656ff. Cited on page76 of *The Abolition of Marriage,* by Maggie Gallagher

"Ten percent of children of divorce will go on to witness three or more family breakups."
Peterson, "Marital Disruption," 5. Cited on page76 of *The Abolition of Marriage,* by Maggie Gallagher

The consequences of divorce often last for many years. One of the most disturbing outcomes arises when young children of divorce reach their young adult years and have difficulty creating trusting and secure intimate relationships.

Judith Wallerstein, Julia Lewis, and Sandra Blakeslee, *The Unexpected Legacy of Divorce: A 25 Year Landmark Study* (New York: Hyperion, 2000), p.304-305.

Only 12% of divorced couples are able to create low-conflict, friendly, relationships after divorce. One-half engage in bitter, open conflict. Five years afterwards, most of these angry divorced couples remain bogged down in hostility. Almost 33% of friendly divorces deteriorate into open conflict.

Constance Ahrons, The Good Divorce: Keeping Your Family Together When Your Marriage Comes Apart (Harper Collins Publications, 1994)

Children of Divorce Getting Divorced

White female children of divorce are 60% more likely to personally experience divorce or separation than a similar population from intact families. The rate for white male children is 35% higher than for similar males from intact families.

Brian Willats, *Breaking Up is Easy To Do,* available from Michigan Family Forum, citing N.D. Glenn and K.B. Kramer, "The marriages and divorces of the children of divorce," Journal of Marriage and the Family, 49, pp. 811-825. Cited in Judith Wallerstein, Ph.D., "The Long-Term Effects of Divorce on Children: A Review," Journal of the American Academy of Child and Adolescent Psychiatry, May 1991, p. 357.

Financial Costs

"Divorce can be quite expensive. If you're

lucky and if both the spouses and their lawyers are reasonable and fair you can get a custody divorce for under $10,000 per spouse in lawyer fees. It is considered unethical for a divorce lawyer to give a client an estimate. A custody fight can be more like $20,000 per spouse or more. After the resolution, either side can return to court the next year to try the case all over again. You could be struggling over the visitation provisions until the children are grown."

http://patriot.net/~crouch/artj/tvshow.html#anchor1530811 John Crouch, Executive Director Americans for Divorce Reform divorcereform@usa net, Arlington, Virginia

"A single divorce costs state and federal governments about $30,000, based on such things as the higher use of food stamps and public housing as well as increased bankruptcies and juvenile delinquency. The nation's 10.4 million divorces in 2002 are estimated to have cost the taxpayers over $30 billion."

Whitehead, B. and Popenoe, D. The State of Our Unions.
Feburary 25, 2006
http://marriage.rutgers.edu/Publications/SOOU/SOOU2004. pdf

Poverty

"Daughters who divorce require far more finan-cial aid from their aging parents than do their married sisters."

Glenna Spitze, "Adult Children's Divorce and Intergenerational Relationships," Journal of Marriage and the Family (May 1994): 279ff. Cited on page 44 of *The Abolition of Marriage*, by Maggie Gallagher

"In Utah, divorce and its financial stresses account for 75 to 80 percent of the people on welfare rolls."
"Utah's Unique Take on How to Strengthen Marriages" by Katharine Biele in The Christian Science Monitor 9/19/98

"Children whose parents divorce are almost twice as likely to drop into poverty than they were before the marital split."
Brian Willats, Breaking Up is Easy To Do, available from Michigan Family Forum, citing Suzanne Bianchi and Edith McArthur, Family Disruption and Economic Hardship, U.S. Census Bureau, 1991. Cited in Kenneth Jost and Marilyn Robinson, "Children and Divorce: What can be done to help children of divorce," CQ Researcher, June 7,1991, p. 358

"Divorce increases the father's odds of winding up in a low occupational stratum, and has decreased a family's ability to pass advantages on to their children."
Timothy J. Biblarz and Adrian E. Raftery, "The Effects of Family Disruption on Social Mobility," American Sociological Review 58 (1993): 97-109. Cited on page 44 of *The Abolition of Marriage,* by Maggie Gallagher

"The average child from a middle class family will suffer a 50% drop in income after divorce."
Sara McLanahan and Gary Sandefur, Growing Up with a Single Parent: What Hurts, What Helps (Cambridge, Mass. Harvard University Press, 1994), 24. Cited on page 32 of The Abolition of Marriage, by Maggie Gallagher

Mental Health
The National Institute of Mental Health found that

annual depression rates for divorced women were over 2.7 times greater than married and never divorced women. Suffering from *any* psychiatric disorder over a lifetime is significantly lower for those in a legal marriage. Lee Robins and Darrel Regier, *Psychiatric Disorders in America: The Epidemiologic Catchment Area Study* (New York: Free Press, 1991), p. 64

Children living with divorced mothers receive professional help for emotional or behavioral problems 3.25 times more than children living with both natural parents. Children living with mothers and stepfathers receive professional help for emotional or behavioral problems 2.44 times more than children living with both natural parents.
Deborah A. Dawson, "Family Structure and Children's Health and Well-Being: Data from the 1988 National Heath Interview Survey on Child Health," *Journal of Marriage and the Family,* 1991, 53:578

"Married people suffered from schizophrenia, depression or any mental illness less often than the unmarried and when they did, their recovery was more successful. The lowest rates for mental hospital admissions were consistently found among the married."
Robert H. Coombs, "Marital Status and Personal Well-Being: A Literature Review," Family Relations, 1991, 40:99

Children living with mom and dad received professional help for behavior and psychological problems at half the rate of children not living with both biological parents.

Deborah A. Dawson, "Family Structure and Children's Health and Well-being: Data from the National Health Interview Survey on Child Health," Journal of Marriage and the Family, 1991,53:573-584

Ten years after their parent's divorce, almost half the children were "worried, underachieving, self-deprecating and sometimes angry." Serious emotional and relational problems follow children of divorce into adulthood.

Judith S. Wallerstein and Sandra Blakeslee, Second Chances: Men, Women, and Children a Decade After Divorce (New York: Ticknor & Fields, 1990) pp. 352-353

The divorced are nearly twice as likely to suffer from any mental illness as those who are married.

Lee Robins and Darrel Regier, Psychiatric Disorders in America: The Epidemiologic Catchment Area Study (New York: Free Press, 1991), p.44.

"Compared to the married, divorced persons are six to ten times more likely to use inpatient psychiatric facilities and four to five times more likely to be clients in outpatient clinics."

David Williams, et al., "Marital Status and Psychiatric Disorders Among Black and Whites," Journal of Health and Social Behavior, 1992, 33:140-157.

"Children of divorce were four times more likely than children in intact families to say they had problems with peers and friends."

The Abolition of Marriage, by Maggie Gallagher p. 65, citing

Dorothy Tysse and Margaret Crosbie-Burnett, "Moral Dilemmas of Early Adolescents of Divorced and Intact Families: A Qualitative and Quantitative Analysis," Journal of Early Adolescence 13, no. 2 (May 1993): 168-182.

Children from divorced families are more isolated than children from stable marriages. They depend more on teachers, counselors, and baby-sitters for support while at the same time perceiving these 'outsiders' as sources of family conflict. The children from divorced families are also more dissatisfied with the support they receive from friends.

Sylvie Drapeau and C. Bouchard, "Support Networks and Adjustment Among 6 to 11 Year Olds from Marital Disrupted and Intact Families," Journal of Divorce and Remarriage 19 (1993):75-97.

"Children of divorce were more aggressive than children whose parents stayed married."

Robert E. Emery, Marriage, Divorce, and Children's Adjustment (Newbury Park, Calif.: Sage Publication, 1988), 50-54.

"Children in homes with absent fathers are more likely to suffer from Attention Deficit Hyperactivity Disorder. No reduction in child antisocial behavior is associated with acquiring a stepfather."

Pfiffner, L., McBurnett, K., Rathouz, P. (2001) Father Absence and Familial Antisocial Charecteristics. *Journal of Abnormal Child Psychology.* v29 i5 p357

"Young children whose parents divorced were likely to be afflicted with emotional problems such as depression or anxiety well into their twenties or

early thirties."
Maher, B. (2003) Patching Up the American Family. *World and* I, v18 it p56.

"Having dealt extensively with both adults who were the product of divorced parents and others who suffered abuse in the early years, I have come to the sad conclusion that the traumatic effects of divorce on the young persons' mind and emotions are significantly greater than those of childhood abuse."
Dr Neil Stringer, New Hope Family Care, Sanford, Florida

Suicide

"The highest suicide rates occur among the divorced, and lowest among the married."
Robert H. Coombs, "Marital Status and Personal Well-Being: A Literature Review," Family Relations, 1991, 40:97-98.

"Of many variables, divorce had the strongest direct relationship to suicide rates."
Jeffery Barr, et al., "Catholic Religion and Suicide: The Mediating Effect of Divorce," Social Science Quarterly, 1994, 75:300-318.

"Divorced individuals are three times more likely to commit suicide than those who are married."
Dick Smith, et al., "Marital Status and the Risk of Suicide," American Journal of Public Health, 1988,78:78-80.

"The suicide rate for divorced white men, is

four times higher than for their married counterparts."
Quoted in Bryce J. Christensen, "In Sickness and in Health: The Medical Costs of Family Meltdown," Policy Review, Spring 1992, p. 71

Physical Health

"The general health problems of children from broken homes are increased by 20 to 30%, even when adjusting for demographic variables."
L. Remez, "Children Who Don't Live with Both Parents Face Behavioral Problems," Family Planning Perspectives, January/ February 1992.

The National Center for Health Statistics finds that married women suffer half the injuries of divorced women.
Robert Coombs, "Marital Status and Personal Well-Being: A Literature Review," Family Relations, 1991, 40:97-102.

"Divorced men are over 9 times more likely to die of tuberculosis and over 4 times more likely to die from diabetes than their married counterparts. A divorced male is 3.4 times more likely to die from any cause than a married male and a divorced female is 2.0 times more likely to die from any cause then her married counterpart."
Walter Gove, "Sex, Marital Status and Mortality," American Journal of Sociology, 1973,79:45-67.

"Being divorced and a non-smoker is slightly less dangerous than smoking a pack or more a day and staying married."

Quoted in Bryce J. Christensen, "In Sickness and in Health: The Medical Costs of Family Meltdown," Policy Review, Spring 1992, p. 71. Cited in Brian Willats, Breaking Up is Easy To Do, available from Michigan Family Forum.

"Divorced men and women suffer to a much greater degree than married persons early death from cancer, cardiovascular disease, strokes, pneumonia, hypertension, and suicide. The single most powerful predictor of stress-related physical illness is marital disruption."

Brian Willats, *Breaking Up is Easy To Do,* available from Michigan Family Forum. Citing B.M. Rosen, H.F. Goldsmith, and R.W. Rednick, Demographic and Social Indicators from the U.S. Census of Population and Housing: Uses for Mental Health Planning in Small Areas (Rockville, MD: National Institute of Mental Health, 1977). Cited in Susan Larson and David Larson, M.D., M.S.P.H., "Divorce: A Hazard to Your Health?" Physician, May/June 1990, p. 14.

"Married people enjoy greater longevity than the unmarried and generally make less use of health care services. Cures from cancer were 8-17% more likely for the married and they also spend fewer days in bed due to acute illness."

Robert H. Coombs, "Marital Status and Personal Well-Being: A Literature Review," Family Relations, 1991, 40:98

"Those who lived alone or with someone other than a spouse had significantly shorter survival times compared with those living with a spouse...the critical factor for survival was the presence of a spouse."

Maradee A. Davis, John M. Neuhaus, Deborah J. Moritz and Mark R. Segal, "Living Arrangements and Survival among Middle-Aged and OlderAdults in the NHANES I Epidemiologic Follow-up Study," American Journal of Public Health, 1992, 82:401-406.

"Married people have the lowest morbidity rates, while the divorced show the highest."

I. M. Joung, et al., "Differences in Self-Reported Morbidity by Marital Status and by Living Arrangement," International Journal of Epidemiology, 1994, 23:91-97.

"Children who come from divorced families are more likely to be shorter. Stress is linked to the hippocampus and growth hormones, learning and memory."

Quote from Diane Sollee, Director of the Coalition for Marriage, Family and Couples Education, from the Coalition's listserv (http://lists.his.com/smartmarriages/)

Alcoholism

Separated and divorced individuals account for 70 percent of all chronic problem drinkers, while married drinkers account for only 15 percent. Single men are over 3 times more likely to die of cirrhosis of the liver than married men.

Robert H. Coombs, "Marital Status and Personal Well-Being: A Literature Review," Family Relations, 1991, 40:97

"Alcoholism rates for divorced or separated individuals are 1.8 times higher than those with intact marriages." Alcoholism rates for those divorced more than once increases to 2.7 times higher than those with intact marriages.

Lee Robins and Darrel Regier, *Psychiatric Disorders in America: The Epidemiologic Catchment Area Study* (New York: Free Press, 1991), p. 103.

Crime

"Criminologists have long used race and poverty as key variables for explaining crime rates. However, when differences in family structures are taken into account, crime rates run much the same in rich and poor neighborhoods and among black, white, and Hispanic populations."

Douglas A. Smith and G. Roger Jarjoura, "Social Structure and Criminal Victimization," Journal of Research in Crime and Delinquency 25 [Feb., 1988], 27-52; epitomizing in The Family in America: New Research, June 1988 Cited in Amneus, The Garbage Generation, page 220

Seventy-two percent of incarcerated juveniles came from broken homes. A child growing up in a divorced family is seven times as likely to be a delinquent.

Statistics from the Los Angeles Times, 19 September, 1988. Cited in Amneus, The Garbage Generation, page 179

More than two-thirds of domestic violence offenders are boyfriends or ex-spouses, while just 9 percent are first spouses.

Gallagher in "End No-Fault Divorce?" (Maggie Gallagher debates Barbara Dafoe Whitehead) in *First Things 75* (August/ September 1997)

Juvenile delinquency in broken homes is 10-15 percent higher than in intact homes.

Edward L. Wells and Joseph H. Rankin, "Families and Delinquency: A Meta-Analysis of the Impact of Broken Homes," Social Problems, 1991,38:71-89.

"Comparing two groups of young black males, another study found that one group is significantly more likely to be sent to jail. Both groups lived in public housing, were on welfare and had similar life experiences. The only difference was the law abiding males had both parents present in the home."

M. Anne Hill and June O'Neill. Underclass Behaviors in the United States: Measurements and Analysis of Determinants (New York: City University of New York, Baruch College, 1993) p. 90.

"If you look at the one factor that most closely correlates with crime, it's not poverty, it's not employment, and it's not education. It's the absence of the father in the family." - U.S. Attorney General William Barr

Wade Horn, Father Facts, The National Fatherhood Initiative, 1995, p. 23.

From 1973 to 1993, divorced women were victims of violent crimes over 4 times more than married women.

U.S. Bureau of Justice Statistics, Highlights from 20 years of Surveying Crime Victims: The National Crime Victimization Survey, 1973-1992 (Washington, D.C.: U.S. Department of Justice, 1993), 18.

Education

Children from divorced families are over 70% more likely than those living with both natural parents to have been expelled or suspended.

Deborah A. Dawson, "Family Structure and Children's Health and Well-being: Data from the National Health Interview Survey on Child Health," Journal of Marriage and the Family, 53, p. 578.

One-third of affluent divorced fathers chose to help pay for college. Ten years after their parents divorce, 60 percent of young adults were on a downward educational course compared with their fathers.

Judith S. Wallerstine and Sandra Blakeskee, *Second Chances:Men Women, and Children a Decade After Divorce* (New York: Ticknor & Fields, 1989), 156-157.

The number one factor that kept children from doing well in school was a broken family. The family health was a greater influence than school facilities, curriculum or staff.

James S. Coleman, et al., Equality of Educational Opportunity, U.S. Department of Health, Education and Welfare, Washington D.C.,1966.

"Researchers from Johns Hopkins and

Princeton Universities found that growing up in a single-parent family had a negative effect on grade-point average, school attendance, and general indicators of educational attainment."
Nan Marie Astone and Sarah S. McLanahan, "Family Structure, Parental Practices and High School Completion," American Sociological Review, 1991,56:309-320.

Children from low-income intact families outperform students from high-income single parent homes!
"One-Parent Families and Their Children: The School's Most Significant Minority," conducted by The Consortium for the Study of School Needs of Children from One-Parent Families, cosponsored by the National Association of Elementary School Principals and the Institute for Development of Educational Activities, a division of the Charles F. Kettering Foundation (Arlington, VA: 1980).

Children from broken homes are nearly twice as likely to drop out of school as those living with both natural parents.
Sara McLanahan and Gary Sandefur, Growing Up with a Single Parent: What Hurts, What Helps, (Cambridge: Harvard University Press, 1994), p. 41.

Illegitimacy

Young white women raised in broken homes are over 2.5 times more likely to bear children out of wedlock themselves.
I. Garfinkel, and S. S. McLanahan,. Single Mothers and Their Children: A New American Dilemma (Washington D.C.: The Urban Institute Press, 1986) pp. 30-31.

Children of divorce are far more likely to engage in premarital sex and bear children out of wedlock during adolescence and young adulthood.
Maher, B. (2003) Patching Up the American Family. World and I, v 18 i 1 p56. Retrieved June 9, 2004 from Expanded Academic ASAP

Religion

Children of divorced Catholic parents are 2.2 times as likely to apostatize. Children of divorced moderate Protestants are 2.2 times as likely to reject all religion. Children of divorced conservative Protestants are 2.7 times as likely to leave Christianity.
Lawton, L. E., & Bures, R. (2001). Parental Divorce and the "Switching" of Religious Identity. Journal for the Scientific Study of Religion, 40, 99-111.

Thirty-seven percent of young adults from divorced families say that religion doesn't speak to the significant questions in their lives, compared to 29% from whole families. Forty-six percent of young adults from divorced families believe that they can find truth without religion, compared to 36% from intact families.
Elizabeth Marquardt *Between Two Worlds: The Inner Lives of Children of Divorce* (New York: Crown Publishers, 2005) 154

Sixty-six percent of those regularly attending religious services at the time of their parent's divorce report that no one from either the clergy or the congregation attempted to minister to them.
Leora E. Lawton and Regina Bures, "Parental Divorce and the

'Switching' of Religious Identity," *Journal for the Scientific Study of Religion,* March 2001, 106 cited on page 155 of *Between Two Worlds: The Inner Lives of Children of Divorce,* by Elizabeth Marquardt

Step-Families

Both teens in single-parent families and teens in step-families are three times more likely to have needed psychological help within the past year.
Peter Hill, "Recent Advances in Selected Aspects of Adolescent Development," Journal of Child Psychology and Psychiatry 34, no. 1 (1993): 69-99. Cited on page 72 of *The Abolition of Marriage,* by Maggie Gallagher

"Living in a mother/stepfather family has as much negative effect as living in a mother only family."
Furstenberg and Cherlin, Divided Families, 77. Cited on page72 of *The Abolition of Marriage,* by Maggie Gallagher

Furstenberg and Cherlin found that "disturbed adolescent functioning" is as common among teens of stepfamilies as in teens of single-parent families, and much more common than in intact families. Thus, it is concluded that remarriage does nothing for the psychological well-being of adolescents.
Furstenberg and Cherlin, Divided Families, 89. Cited on page 72 of *The Abolition of Marriage,* by Maggie Gallagher

"It appears that children in stepfamilies have the same frequency of problems as do children in single-parent families."
Jiang Hong Li and Roger A. Wojtkiewicz, "A New Look at the Effects of Family Structure on Status Attainment," Social Science Quarterly 73 (1992): 581-595. Cited on page72 of *The Abolition of*

Marriage, by Maggie Gallagher

"Remarriage turned up in a study to be more unstable than the first marriage."
See for example,Andrew Cherlin, "Remarriage as an Incomplete Institution," American Journal of Sociology 84 (1978): 634ff; Frank F. Furstenberg, Jr., and Graham B. Spanier, Recycling the Family: Remarriage After Divorce (Beverly Hills, Calif.: Sage Publications, 1987), 86-90. Cited on page71 of *The Abolition of Marriage,* by Maggie Gallagher

"Children in stepfamilies do no better on average than children in single-parent homes."
J.A. Jacobs and Frank F. Furstenberg, Jr., "Changing Places: Conjugal Careers and Women's Marital Mobility," Social Forces 64: 714ff. Cited on page71 of *The Abolition of Marriage,* by Maggie Gallagher

"A study by James Bray, of the Baylor College of Medicine, Houston, reveals that stepchildren have about twice the rate of serious behavioral problems as children in traditional nuclear families."
Marilyn Elias, "A 'Boomerang' Among Stepkids," USA Today, August 17, 1998.

"Children living with both biological parents usually manage better than children in any other family form, including step families. The advantage of marriage seems to exist mainly when the child is the biological offspring of both parents."
Manning, Wendy, & Lamb, Kathleen A. (2003). Adolescent well-being in cohabiting, married, and singleparent families. *Journal of Marriage & Family,* 65: 890

Does any of this, in any way, represent the "Fruit of the Spirit?" Do any of these statistics manifest, in any way, the pure lifestyle of Jesus Christ? Should any of these results be present in the lives of those who profess Jesus Christ as Lord and Savior? Yet, this is the horrible fruit of present day teaching concerning divorce and remarriage in most churches. This distorted teaching being espoused, has caused the divorce and remarriage rate in our churches to soar higher than the level in the un-churched world and Pastors and their wives are now one of the highest segments of our society to be experiencing divorce and remarriage. Brothers and sisters, these things ought not to be. There is a Trojan Horse in the Church and it can only be dealt with when God's people recognize it, and do battle against it.

Jesus said in John 8:32, *"And ye shall know the Truth, and the Truth shall make you free."* May we suggest in this situation it might make you miserable at first, but eventually you will know a new freedom of spirit, mind and conscience because it is Biblical truth.

As a church, we should be asking; with all of this statistical evidence available to Christian leaders today, why are none calling for a reevaluation of the marriage doctrine? Why is the divorce problem moving through the congregations and into the pulpits with less and less opposition? Why are our protestant churches still stubbornly embracing

Why are none calling for a reevaluation of the marriage doctrine?

this Trojan Horse? This ungodly doctrine destroys our witness to the world and exposes the hypocrisy of those who oppose sodomy, but wholeheartedly embrace the violence being done in the Christian community by divorce and remarriage.

Please do not accuse the Holy Spirit of birthing this corrupt fruit that has caused devastation within the Church. The Church must recognize this Trojan Horse ideology that was introduced by a humanistic, rationalist who violated every hermeneutic principle to arrive at his conclusions. The Trojan Horse's five word school-*"except it be for fornication"*-is eroding our Christian society while church leadership defends it. Regardless of the cost, we must go back to the only true source of authority, the eternal Word of God. May God raise up courageous leaders in the Church who are willing to research this for themselves and restore true New Testament teaching on marriage and divorce.

Let's look again at our Lord's teaching and embrace it.

Chapter 5

Clear Bible Passages On Divorce and Remarriage
❧❧

The Proper Interpretation of Scripture

The first prerequisite in knowing any biblical truth is to establish a sound scriptural premise. Any argument, even if it seems like a strong argument, if based upon a false premise, is error, no matter how logical or pleasant it sounds. Our present day doctrine, based upon a false premise, is already producing bitter water, bad fruit and moral decay in our families.

The first two rules of proper interpretation of

Scripture are:

❖ Establish a scriptural premise. This means to find as many Scripture verses as you can that agree and use them as a basis for establishing a doctrine.

❖ Passages that seem unclear should be interpreted in the light of passages that are clear. Then a verdict can be rendered.[xxv] If the prevailing doctrinal foundation being promoted in much of our Christian culture today contains errors; it will become very difficult for anyone to come to a biblical worldview.

Any worldview in the Church other than a biblical worldview is destined for spiritual destruction. Jesus spoke of the importance of a proper foundation in Matthew chapter seven:

And everyone that heareth these sayings (words) of mine, and doeth them not, shall be likened unto a foolish man, which built his house upon the sand; and the rain descended, and the floods came, and the winds blew, and beat upon that house; and it fell: and great was the fall of it. Matthew 7:26, 27.

Properly presenting Christ's saying is one of the most critical tasks any servant of Christ ever faces.

If we distort His words, the Church will ultimately suffer damages.

Let's remind ourselves again of a vital premise; principles of sound biblical interpretation are best preserved when scriptural passages which seem unclear are interpreted in the light of those passages which are clear. If we compare and evaluate Scripture with Scripture, we find the Bible to be its own best commentary. One rule of comparing Scripture, which

> All obscure and seemingly contradictory verses must submit to those verses which are clear and concise.

must not be disregarded is; the plain verses are the main verses. All obscure and seemingly contradictory verses must submit to those verses which are clear and concise. If this method is faithfully followed, the unclear, or obscure and seemingly contradictory verses will become clear and harmonious with the clear verses and a sound verdict can be rendered.

If you read the majority of materials available on marriage, divorce and remarriage in Christian book stores, you could very easily come away with writings to support any number of opinions. Most however are based upon life experience and opinions and are not totally based upon scripture. Most present day books begin and end with the Erasmian Theory, which is today called the Matthew/Pauline exception theory. This theory is an attempt to explain a verse of Scripture which we choose to label as an unclear verse. These same present day books then proceed to explain away the clear Scripture passages as being irrelevant or incomplete. This is why we believe it is very important for us to realize this theory was not devised in the New Testament nor by the earliest Church fathers, but in the sixteenth century, by Desiderius Erasmus; and was then perpetuated and enlarged upon by the Reformers.

When the "exception Scripture passages" are honestly compared to the clear passages, containing no exceptions, they seem to contradict the clear passages. If we are to build a truly Biblical basis for this subject, it is imperative we understand what the clear passages say first, and then compare them with the seemingly contradictive verses, which Erasmus "re-interpreted."

Before we can determine an answer to the divorce problem in our society, we must go back to the foundation; the very beginning; to the actual institution of marriage. If we miss or distort the pure teaching here in the slightest degree, we will be building beautiful castles in the sky of men's ideas, with no authoritative foundation. Any valid solution must be based solely upon the complete revelation in God's Word, which also requires beginning at the beginning, comparing Scripture with Scripture and reevaluating all we have assumed in the past.

Old Testament:

Genesis 2: 21-24
In the Beginning: The inception of marriage.
And the LORD God caused a deep sleep to fall upon Adam, and he slept: and he took one of his ribs, and closed up the flesh instead thereof; And the rib, which the LORD God had taken from man, made he a woman, and brought her unto the man. And Adam said, This is now bone of my bones, and flesh of my flesh: she shall be called Woman, because she was taken out of Man. Therefore shall a man leave his father and his mother, and shall cleave unto his wife: and they shall be one flesh. Genesis 2:21-24

From this portion of Scripture, we can clearly see God intended one man and one woman to have a *"one flesh"* relationship for life. They were to leave their parents and *"cleave"* or be glued to each other; with no acknowledgement of separation or divorce whatsoever.

When Adam spoke his words of acceptance, God immediately spoke up and said, *"Therefore..."* Something very significant had just taken place which caused God, the Creator, to say, *"Therefore shall a man leave his father and mother, and shall cleave unto his wife: and they shall be one flesh."* Adam's verbal receiving of Eve established the first marriage covenant, which caused the Creator to supernaturally make them *"one flesh"* for life. The prophet, Malachi, affirms this fact.

Malachi 2:13-16 God hates divorce.

> *And this have ye done again, covering the altar of the LORD with tears, with weeping, and with crying out, insomuch that he regardeth not the offering any more, or receiveth it with good will at your hand. Yet ye say, Wherefore? Because the LORD hath been witness between thee and the wife of thy youth, against whom thou hast dealt treacherously: yet is she thy companion, and the wife of thy covenant. And did not he make one? Yet had he the residue of the spirit. And wherefore one? That he might seek a godly seed. Therefore take heed to your spirit, and let none deal treacherously against the wife of his youth. For the LORD, the God of Israel, saith that he hateth putting away: for one covereth violence with his garment, saith the LORD of hosts: therefore take heed to your spirit, that ye deal not treacherously. Malachi 2:13-16*

In this passage we see:
- God did not accept the sacrifices of these Jews because they divorced their wives.
- Marriage is established by a verbal

covenant.^{xxvi}

- God hates divorce.
- Divorce and remarriage always produces negative spiritual and social repercussions.

In the above portion of Scripture we find the Lord God speaking through His servant, Malachi, to a people immersed in confusion and consternation because of their failure to obey His standards concerning marriage. This scene is reminiscent of Samuels' confrontation with King Saul, when Saul refused to wait for the prophet to arrive before offering the required sacrifices to the Lord.

When Saul attempted to make excuses for his impatience, Samuel reminded him of a divine principle we all should be reminded of today: *"...Behold, to obey is better than sacrifice." I Samuel 15:22*

New Testament Gospels

Jesus said to his disciples,

*"Whosoever shall put away his wife **except it be for fornication** and shall marry another, committeth adultery." Matthew 5:32*

Jesus told the Pharisees,

*"Whosoever shall put away (divorce) his wife, **except it be for fornication,** and shall marry another, committeth adultery; and whoso marrieth her which is put away (divorced) doth commit*

adultery." Matthew 19:9

Tempting Jesus

> *And the Pharisees came to him, and asked him, Is it lawful for a man to put away his wife? tempting him. And he answered and said unto them, What did Moses command you? And they said, Moses suffered to write a bill of divorcement, and to put her away. And Jesus answered and said unto them, For the hardness of your heart he wrote you this precept. But from the beginning of the creation God made them male and female. For this cause shall a man leave his father and mother, and cleave to his wife; And they twain shall be one flesh: so then they are no more twain, but one flesh. What therefore God hath joined together, let not man put asunder. And in the house his disciples asked him again of the same matter. And he saith unto them, Whosoever shall put away his wife, and marry another, committeth adultery against her. And if a woman shall put away her husband, and be married to another, she committeth adultery. Mark 10: 2-12*

On several occasions, the Gospel writers recorded how the Jewish religious leaders tried to trap Jesus. We see in the Scripture above how Mark recorded a particular incident when the Pharisees attempted to entrap Jesus concerning the subject of divorce. These men wanted Him to take sides with either the liberal divorce group of Rabbi Hillel, or the conservative group of Rabbi Shammai. These two groups disagreed over the interpretation of Moses' words in Deuteronomy 24.

It was very interesting to see how Jesus' answer completely disregarded both Hillel, and Shammai. He even bypassed Moses, along with the Pharisees's interpretation of Moses, by stating a husband and wife are not to remarry under any circumstances. Later on, when the disciples asked about this teaching, He clearly declared, any husband who divorces his wife and remarries while his wife is still alive, commits adultery. He then made it even stronger by saying any wife who divorces her husband and remarries while her husband is still alive, commits adultery; with no exceptions.

Luke 16:18

Jesus said to the Jewish leaders (Pharisees), *"Whosoever putteth away* (divorces) *his wife, and marrieth another, **committeth adultery:** and whosoever marrieth her that is put away from her husband committeth adultery." Luke 16:18* Please note again there is no exception here; unlike what is seemingly found in Matthew 5:27-32 and 19:3-9, *"except it be for fornication."*

91

We could paraphrase what Jesus said in Luke by saying: If anyone **ever,** for **any reason,** divorces their wife or husband and marries another, **they are committing adultery,** with no exceptions and no ambiguity. Remember, without exception this is what all of the earliest Church fathers believed.

The first word to note in this verse is *"Whosoever."* This same word is found in John 3:16, and applies to all mankind, thus giving this truth universal application. This particular application, as in John 3:16, applies to any offspring of Adam and Eve, Christian or non-Christian.

To illustrate what Jesus was very clearly saying, we could say: if Dick and Jane are married and Dick divorces Jane and marries Sally; the remarriage is not a marriage at all, but constitutes adultery in God's sight.

If adultery is sex outside the marriage bond with someone other than your original spouse, then Jesus is saying Dick's act of divorcing Jane and marrying Sally, did not BREAK the original covenant marriage bond; it only violated it. Most people today would say Dick divorced Jane and is now married to Sally. Today this would be considered a typical divorce and remarriage. We must see these actions through God's eyes, because Jesus said Dick and Jane were still one flesh, and therefore, by Dick marrying Sally; *"They committeth adultery,"* according to Jesus' words in *Luke 16:18*. This clearly reveals Dick was having a sexual relationship with someone other than his wife, Jane, and called the new relationship, "adultery."

After Dick divorced Jane and married Sally; Jesus said Dick was committing ADULTERY against Jane. Jesus extended this reasoning another step, by adding; if Tom comes along and marries Jane, who has already been divorced by Dick and is considered the "innocent" party; Tom would also be committing adultery and causing Jane to commit adultery against Dick as well. By Tom marrying Jane they both became adulterers.

Let's read it again: *"And whosoever* (Tom) *marrieth her* (Jane) *that is put away* (divorced) *from her husband* (Dick), *committeth adultery."* This is Christ's conclusion because in God's sight, the marriage covenant between Dick and Jane is still valid until death. Like Dick, Jane would be having sexual relations with someone other than her covenant husband. Remember, the Lord Jesus Himself said this without adding any exceptions whatsoever.

This verse (Luke 16:18) when taken at face value, tells us God hears, honors and supernaturally acts upon the first marriage vows any previously unmarried man and woman make to each other, by binding them as *"one flesh"* for life. By doing so, God considers meaningless any future divorce or multiple marriage certificates. They are forbidden and totally unrecognizable or acceptable in His sight. Other examples of "forbidden marriages" include:

- A mother with her son.
- A father with his daughter.

- A man with a man.
- A woman with a woman.
- Any remarriage while one's first partner is still alive.

For God to recognize new vows with Dick and Sally or Tom and Jane, He would have to violate His own holiness, righteousness and justice. God set the terms of the marriage covenant; it is *"till death."*

No other conclusion of this portion of Scripture can be reached if interpreted in its most natural and logical meaning. If we interpret it any other way, we must also say the disciples' response to what they heard Jesus say was a monumental overreaction: *"If the case of the man be so with his wife, it is not good to marry." Matthew 19:10* If Christ meant that it was okay to divorce and remarry, then the disciples totally overreacted.

Jesus declares:

"For this cause shall a man leave father and mother, and shall cleave to his wife: and they twain shall be one flesh. Wherefore, they are no more twain but one flesh. What therefore God hath joined together (literally glued together), let not man put asunder." Matthew 19:5-6

The Living Bible says: *"And no man may divorce what God has joined together."*

New Testament
Epistles Romans 7:2,3
The Law of Marriage

For the woman which hath an husband is bound by the law to her husband so long as he liveth; but if the husband be dead, she is loosed from the law of her husband. So then if, while her husband liveth, she be married to another man, she shall be called an adulteress: but if her husband be dead, she is free from that law; so that she is no adulteress, though she be married to another man. Romans 7:2-3

Many people say Paul wasn't speaking about marriage in this passage as they try to justify remarriage. These same people fail to realize they are repeating Erasmus' and Luther's rationalizations, and not Scripture. Not one of the earliest church fathers ever believed or taught this.

Such an interpretation scripturally, contextually and exegetically does not hold water. Paul was comparing how the Law (Decalogue) was applicable to any person until they died just like the marriage covenant is in effect until one or the other married person dies. Paul clearly teaches in this passage that marriage is for life, declaring, anyone who gets remarried while their spouse is still alive is considered an adulteress or an adulterer.

- This is what Paul consistently believed and taught.
- Is this what your church teaches?

- Is this what you believe and teach?
- Is this what your life demonstrates?

I Corinthians 7:10, 11
Paul on Marriage

*And unto the married I command, yet not I,
but the Lord, Let not the wife depart from
her husband: But and if she depart, let her
remain unmarried, or be reconciled to her
husband: and let not the husband put away
his wife.*
I Corinthians 7:10-11

Again, Paul clearly teaches a woman must either
be reconciled to her husband or live alone. He does
not even suggest she find another husband. He also
says that a man is not to even consider divorcing his
wife. It should be noted here, this portion is
applicable in reverse, inasmuch as a wife should not
divorce her husband and if a husband leaves, he
should also remain unmarried, or be reconciled to
his wife. This dual responsibility is affirmed in
Mark 10: 11, 12.

- Is this what you believe, teach and
  practice?
- This is what the New Testament teaches.

Chapter 6

Understanding Biblical Covenants
❦❦

Don't Confuse Sin With A Covenant:

Another pervasive doctrine permeating the
Church today is the practice of calling divorce and
remarriage just "a sin." Divorce and remarriage is
not just an act of sin. Paul said it is a state of being
and titles the person as *"an adulteress."* In *Luke
16:18,* Jesus explained such an act, not as a
remarriage, but as a state of adultery, since divorce
and remarriage does not destroy the covenant; but
only violates it. That violation remains until the
violating partner ceases this adulterous relationship,
or one of the original partners dies. Today's

prevailing theology on this subject says; "If a person has admitted that sin to God, (divorce & remarriage) his/her 'sin' is under the blood and they are now one flesh in the Lord's sight."

This idea is founded upon a misunderstanding of the difference between sin and a covenant. This important difference can best be understood by defining the true structure of a biblical marriage covenant.

Understanding The Marriage Covenant

Marriage, as God established it, is a divine covenant. Once entered into, it is in effect until one partner dies. It is a lifetime covenant, with no exceptions, regardless of what the reformers said. Marriage is a Divine covenant that can be violated, but it cannot be broken by either or both parties and should not be confused with only being an act of sin.

A Flippant Covenant Is Still A Covenant:

When Esau traded his birthright for a *"mess of pottage"* by swearing to his brother Jacob he could have it in exchange for some food. This was two flippant young men, approximately 24 years of age, bantering with each other, seemingly unaware of the seriousness of making a vow before God or what constituted a vow (Genesis 25:29).

The end result of Esau's flippant response to

Jacob is declared in Hebrews: Esau is declared *"a profane person ...who for one morsel of meat sold his birthright. For ye know how that afterward he was rejected: for he found no place of repentance, though he sought it carefully with tears"* Hebrews 12:16-17. God could forgive Esau for his flippancy and stupidity, but it didn't change the birthright or the covenant! What was Esau's birthright, became Jacob's.

It was supposed to be Abraham, Isaac and Esau, except for a few careless words. Those few words completely changed Jewish history. A flippant vow superseded all other considerations. Esau's words created a covenant. That covenant still stands today, as evidenced by the present genealogical order of Abraham, Isaac and Jacob. Today there could be many illustrations given of flippant situations where those involved treat their decision lightly.

One example would be of a couple who meet in Las Vegas. They decide to go to the chapel at 3 a.m. and get married. Later on, they sober up and think they only did a foolish thing that means nothing. They fail to realize they bound themselves flippantly before God and are therefore bound by the marriage law which God established.

It is essential for us today, to recognize the difference between sin and a covenant. Repenting of a violation of the marriage covenant will always result in turning away from that violation and either *"remain unmarried or be reconciled to your husband or wife."* I Corinthians 7:11

A Deceptive Covenant Is Still A Covenant:

Joshua was commanded by God to invade and conquer the Promised Land and to kill all the inhabitants (Joshua 9). The people who lived in the city of Gibea were Amorites, (also called Gibeonites), and were among the tribes inhabiting the land which Joshua had been commanded to destroy.

When the Gibeonites learned Joshua was coming to destroy them, they decided to deceive him and save their lives. To accomplish their trickery, they put on old clothes, took moldy bread, old wineskins, worn out shoes and covered themselves with dust. Then, they rode their camels over the hill to meet Joshua and the people of Israel. When they came before Joshua, they announced they had come from far away to make a peace treaty with Israel. They were lying.

Joshua and his leaders looked at the appearance of the Gibeonites; the condition of their food, clothes, etc., and were convinced they were telling the truth The Bible says; *"they asked not counsel at the mouth of the Lord."* Instead, Joshua 9:15 says: *"And Joshua made peace with them; to let them live: and the princes of the congregation sware unto them."* Almost immediately after this agreement was finalized, someone discovered these emissaries were not from a far away country, but from just over the hill! Joshua and his leaders knew immediately they had been deceived.

Naturally, one would think that Joshua and his

100

leaders would have immediately risen up and killed all of these men for their lies and for making Joshua and the leaders look so foolish. Today's response would likely be, "We were deceived. We didn't know what we were doing. Therefore, there is no covenant." Verse 18 says, *"And the children of Israel smote them not, because the princes of the congregation had sworn unto them by the Lord God of Israel."* Joshua and his tribal leaders knew the seriousness of a verbal vow. They also knew they didn't dare touch the Gibeonites. Instead, from then on Joshua not only let them live, but also protected them from their enemies as he and his men had promised God they would do in their covenant.

The next time we read anything about Israel's covenant with the Gibeonites is 350 years later:

> *Then there was a famine in the days of David three years, year after year; and David enquired of the Lord, and the Lord answered, It is for Saul, and for his bloody house, because he slew the Gibeonites. II Samuel 21:1*

Evidently, Saul was upset because there were so many of the Gibeonites working around the tabernacle and he had some of them killed.

Let's review:

- God originally commanded Joshua to kill all the inhabitants of the land.
- Joshua made a covenant with a group of

deceitful Gibeonites.
- More than 350 years later, Saul kills just a few Gibeonites.
- God brings a severe drought upon the land during David's reign and says it was because Saul had violated Joshua's covenant with the Gibeonites. Saul only <u>violated</u> Joshua's covenant with the Gibeonites by killing them; he didn't break it.

Think about it. God told Joshua to kill all of them, but after a few deceptive words were spoken, everything changed and the Gibeonites became a protected people. Then God punished all of Israel because Saul violated the covenant by killing some Gibeonites. God honors covenants!

David then asked the Lord how he could resolve the problem. The Lord instructed him to go to the leaders of the Gibeonites and ask them what he should do to honorably resolve this violation of the covenant with them and how to make atonement for those Saul had killed.

The law of Israel in that day was, "if a life be taken, a life must be taken." The Gibeonites told David to give them seven of Saul's sons that they might hang them. David turned over seven of Saul's sons and the Gibeonites hanged them.

There is a shocking and enlightening statement found in II Samuel 21:14c: *"And after that* [after Saul's seven sons were hanged] *God was intreated for the land."* After the violated 350 year old covenant was vindicated, God again answered David's prayer and ended the drought.

Imagine how David must have prayed and wept before the Lord during those three years with no results. Relief did not come until restitution to the Gibeonites had been made for Saul's violation (not breaking) of the covenant. Although the covenant (verbal agreement) was crafted in deception, God confirmed it. The words were spoken without seeking God's counsel, but once the covenant was stated in His presence, it was acknowledged, confirmed and enforced by God Himself.

Have you ever heard someone say, "I didn't know what I was saying," or "I didn't understand the seriousness of what I was saying at the time?" God's response is, a covenant is a covenant, between any two qualified individuals, (neither married before, or a widow or widower), and God honors covenants.

Today, individuals contact us asking their status before God, after they agreed to go through the marriage ceremony with someone who wanted to obtain a green card. "It won't be a marriage but a means to an end." If we can deceive the government agencies, we can then get a divorce and move on. These persons go through a legal marriage ceremony; sign all the documents and are pronounced husband and wife in the presence of witnesses, thinking it means nothing. They have fulfilled God's requirements to be made one flesh for life. In the end, they are the ones who were deceived.

Furthermore, if Joshua and the leaders of Israel had met another tribe and made a covenant with them to help them destroy the Gibeonites, it would have been a forbidden covenant and unenforceable by God. This is because the initial covenant was without a time limit and could not be replaced by one that would violate the first covenant.

This is why God will not and cannot recognize a remarriage while either first partner is still living. If he did, He would be violating His own holiness, righteousness, and justice. The terms of the first marriage covenant are for life, regardless.

A Foolish Covenant Is Still A Covenant:

Another good example in Scripture of the seriousness of vows spoken is found in Judges 11. Here we see the story of Jephthah the Gileadite, the son of a harlot.

Because of his mother's reputation, Jephthah and his family were outcasts from Israel's society. When the Ammonites threatened Israel, the people knew that Jephthah was a man of valor. Swallowing their pride, they went to him and asked if he would lead them into battle. After much heart searching, Jephthah agreed and started out to battle. Verse 29 declares, *"the Spirit of the Lord came upon Jephthah;"* which was divine evidence of sure victory. In spite of this evidence Jephthah made a foolish, unnecessary vow before thinking through all of the possible ramifications:

> *And Jephthah vowed a vow unto the LORD, and said, If thou shalt without fail deliver the children of Ammon into mine hands, Then it shall be, that whatsoever cometh forth of the doors of my house to meet me, when I return in peace from the children of Ammon, shall surely be the LORD'S, and I will offer it up for a burnt offering.*
>
> *So Jephthah passed over unto the children of Ammon to fight against them; and the LORD delivered them into his hands."*
> *Judges 11:30-32*

He didn't have to make the vow he made, but he did. We need to put ourselves in Jephthah's shoes and imagine what he was thinking on his way home from battle. We know what some would have been thinking at that time by what they do when they make other promises: "Well, Lord, I know what I said about tithing, but I didn't know the interest rate would go up on my boat loan." Or, "I know I said that I'd preach for You, Lord, but then I didn't realize this scholarship would come along. You understand, Lord." And then there is the excuse, "I know I told You in the jungles of Vietnam or the deserts of Saudi Arabia or Iraq, if You'd get me out alive, I'd serve You the rest of my life. But You understand I was scared then. And besides, I've got a lot of catching up to do." This might be called a situational covenant, made while under duress.

Right here is where many experience spiritual defeat. They have made a vow to God in the past and then forgotten it. God hasn't forgotten. People who make vows and violate them will never know the full joy of an obedient walk until they go back and deal with their vow as Jephthah had to do. Ecclesiastes 5:4-6 warns us, God will *"destroy the work of our hands"* if we say the vow was a mistake and then fail to keep it or renounce the vow we made to Him.

Maybe his thoughts on the way home were something like the following:

"Maybe my wife will be sweeping when I get home and will sweep a chicken out the door. I'll bet old Rover, my hunting dog, will hear me coming and burst out through the door to greet me. Then I can offer the chicken or Rover to the Lord as a burnt offering to fulfill this vow I made."

Please understand...Jephthah never even suggested ignoring his vow. The Word of God says that it didn't happen like that. Instead:

"And Jephthah came to Mizpah unto his house, and, behold, his daughter came out to meet him with timbrels and with dances: and she was his only child." Judges 11:34

Jephthah knew immediately what he had done: *"...I have opened my mouth unto the Lord, and I cannot go back." (vv. 35)*

What did Jephthah vow?

"Then it shall be, that whatsoever cometh forth of the doors of my house to meet me, when I return in peace from the children of Ammon, shall surely be the LORD'S, and I will offer it up for a burnt offering." Judges 11:31

Finally, we read Jephthah's daughter

"...returned unto her father, who did with her according to his vow which he vowed." vv. 39

We are not here to justify or condemn Jephthah because God has already placed him in His Hebrews hall of fame and eulogized him: in vs. *38;* *"Of whom the world was not worthy:"* Hebrews *11:32* Our goal is to show you that a vow to God is a very serious thing. Remember: *"Better is it that thou shouldest not vow, than that thou shouldest vow and not pay."* Ecclesiastes 5:5

There is no other place in Scripture where there may have been a human burnt sacrifice, but there may have been one here simply and profoundly because a man understood the seriousness of his vow to God.

Jephthah cried out; *"I have opened my mouth unto the Lord, and I* ***cannot go back.****" Judges 11:35*

Some say it could not possibly mean that

Jephthah was required to make an actual human burnt offering. They think it means that his daughter

107

would be dedicated for life to temple service. Since it was his only daughter, the punishment would be that she could never marry. Thus, he would have no grandchildren.

The true substance or meaning of his words is not the key issue here. The fact is it was foolish of him to make this unnecessary vow. Jephthah experienced exactly what Solomon said in Proverbs:

Thou art snared with the words of thy mouth,
thou art taken with the words of thy mouth.
Proverbs 6:2

When Jephthah finally realized the tremendous price involved, he was overwhelmed. Despite his agony and grief, he fulfilled the vow. Jephthah knew a vow made to God, whatever the vow might be, must not be broken or rescinded.

A young lady, attending an evangelical Bible college, came to the school with a small child and rented her own apartment. During a week of revival services, this girl stood sobbing before the student body and said:

"I want all of you to know that years ago, I committed my life to serve Christ on the mission field. I ate and slept that dream, until my senior year in high school. Then I met a young man. He wasn't a Christian, but I believed all of Satan's lies and continued on into that relationship. I was warned over and over again. My devotional life slipped away. My prayer life was an array of desperate cries for God to have patience with me while I did my own thing. I sowed to the flesh and reaped corruption. The rest is evident," she said as she motioned toward the small child next to her. "I only hope that somehow, God can still use me on the mission field. Oh, please don't break your promises to God!"

A hush came over the audience. Here was one who had made a vow to God, had violated it, had repented, and was trying to pick up the pieces. We can't help but think that Jephthah wished he hadn't said what he had, but he did.

A modern day example of foolish vows would be applied to where a young lady is found to be pregnant, or a young couple living together out of wedlock.

Well meaning pastors and family members pressure these young people to get married right away. This counsel is based on the belief it will right a wrong. This is not always true, as illustrated by the high percentage of divorces from such situations. Two wrongs do not always make a right.

The pregnant girl should first of all ask the Lord for forgiveness and do nothing more until she is totally convinced the man truly loves, respects and desires to honor and care for her. Up to now, she is not in a covenant and she can recover with her child and go on with her life. She must realize that sex does not create a covenant. If sex created a covenant, then there would be no such thing as a fornicating life-style described in I Corinthians 6:10 and Galatians 5:19. If she marries only because she is pregnant, her life could be negatively affected with no desirable alternative.

The young couple who are pushed to get married, should in reality be urged to repent of their fornication, separate or take the time to see if they are truly compatible in other than physical matters and analyze the level of commitment each are willing to make to the other. This time of analysis would help them consider the seriousness of a permanent and loving relationship, based on love and respect.

To be thrown into a covenant relationship before this would be foolish.

Among the most important lessons we must learn from these illustrations is we can only obey or violate the terms of a covenant made to God; we can never break it. We can say marriage vows before judges, pastors, and Justices of the Peace multiple times, but only the first marriage covenant vow stands before God.

The Church must come to a new awareness of the seriousness of a vow made to God. Furthermore, the Church must teach the warnings to those who violate them. I encourage you to study, meditate upon and pray very carefully over the following verses.

Death and life are in the power of the tongue: and they that love it shall eat the fruit thereof. Proverbs 18:21

And if a man vow a vow unto the LORD, or swear an oath to bind his soul with a bond; he shall not break his word, he shall do according to all that proceedeth out of his mouth. Numbers 30:2

When thou shalt vow a vow unto the LORD thy God, thou shalt not slack to pay it: for the LORD thy God will surely require it of thee; and it would be sin in thee. But if thou shalt forbear to vow, it shall be no sin in thee. That which is gone out of thy lips thou shalt keep and perform; even a freewill offering, according as thou hast vowed unto the LORD thy God, which thou hast promised with thy mouth. Deuteronomy 23:21-23

When thou vowest a vow unto God, defer not to pay it; for he hath no pleasure in fools: pay that which thou hast vowed. Better is it that thou shouldest not vow, than that thou shouldest vow and not pay. Suffer not thy mouth to cause thy flesh to sin; neither say thou before the angel, that it was an error: wherefore should God be

111

angry at thy voice, and destroy the work of thine hands? For in the multitude of dreams and many words there are also divers vanities: but fear thou God. Ecclesiastes 5:4-7

Thou art snared with the words of thy mouth, thou art taken with the words of thy mouth. Proverbs 6:2

Again, ye have heard that it hath been said by them of old time, Thou shalt not forswear thyself, but shalt perform unto the Lord thine oaths: But I say unto you, Swear not at all, neither by heaven for it is God's throne: Nor by the earth; for it is his footstool: neither by Jerusalem; for it is the city of the great King. Neither shalt thou swear by thy head, because thou canst not make one hair white or black. But, let your communication be, Yea, yea; Nay, nay: for whatsoever is more than these cometh of evil. Matthew 5:33-37

If you study the Old Testament carefully, you will notice how God allowed the Jews to make vows in the name of the Lord. Allowed, because making vows was not a commandment. (Deuteronomy 23:22) If someone chose to make a vow and swear, it was to be done in the name of the Lord Jehovah. (Deut 6:13; 10:20)

By making vows and swearing in the name of the Lord, they were calling upon God to be a witness of the commitment being made. By swearing in the name of the Lord, it increased the sense of solemnity and gravity of the promise. It was thought that if a person swore in the name of the Lord, they would be more likely to take their vows more seriously as the Lord would call them into account. (Leviticus 19:12)

As the legalistic Jewish elders continued to teach their legalistic system it evolved to where the seriousness of making a vow was cheapened. They still taught to swear in the name of the Lord absolutely bound the individual to fulfill their promise or commitment, but reasoned and rationalized that obligation to be less binding if the vow was made, swearing by such things as heaven, earth, Jerusalem or one's head. Consequently, they devised formulas allowing persons making vows or oaths, to avoid using the name of the Lord. Over time these became more common than swearing in the name of the Lord. In Jesus' day, a cavalier attitude prevailed when making oaths and vows. The seriousness of making vows had been almost entirely eroded and this is why Jesus sought to restore the original intent of this law.

In Matthew 5:34-36; Jesus condemned the use of non-biblical formulas to evade having to fulfill a vow or oath. In verse 37, He admonishes the listeners to forsake their non-biblical formulas and to be honestly transparent with a simple "yes or no."

We need to understand, Jesus was not calling

for the complete cessation of making oaths and vows or swearing. If he were Paul the Apostle would have been disregarding Christ's own teaching when he provided testimony with an oath: (Acts 18:18) and when calling the Lord as witness in oaths; (Romans 1:9; II Corinthians 1:23; Galatians 1:20). Jesus taught this same foundational principle in Matthew 5:37 and was repeated by James:

> *But above all things, my brethren, swear not, neither by heaven, neither by the earth, neither by any other oath: but let your yea be yea and your nay, nay; lest ye fall into condemnation. James 5:12*

The whole intent of the law, with regard to swearing and vowing was to emphasize the importance of keeping one's word through the fulfillment of one's commitments (Deuteronomy 23:21-23; Psalms 15:4). The Lord's intent in this teaching was not to contradict Moses, but to restore God's original intent and spirit of the law of Moses.

Remember, Erasmus' false doctrine was based on his rationalistic and humanistic training, with no true biblical basis for pure truth. It was a radical teaching, even in his day, which was in the 1500s. The Reformers had just emerged into some light after hundreds of years of spiritual darkness. Remember, of the five positions, the Erasmian View is <u>the only one</u> that declares God allows people to ignore their vows and oaths and divorce and remarry. His teachings were not, and are not founded on a solid exegetical, grammatical or biblical foundation, but on situational ethics and sociological pampering. Like many theologians today, the reformers seemingly ignored and denigrated the four earliest church positions, while enthusiastically embracing the Erasmian view. In so doing, they caused to be fulfilled, the conditions Jesus described in Matthew concerning the last days:

But as the days of Noah were, so shall also the coming of the Son of man be. For as in the days that were before the flood they were eating and drinking, marrying and giving in marriage, until the day that Noah entered into the ark, and knew not until the flood came, and took them all away; so shall also the coming of the Son of man be. Matthew 24:37-39

Many Evangelical Christian leaders who earnestly believe marriage is a life long covenant, find the problem of divorce in their churches overwhelming as they see the social disintegration of church families. These same leaders are desperately trying to find a way to bandage the moral hemorrhage happening in their flocks.

During the past few years, an avalanche of new rationalizations have bombarded the Church to the point where divorce and remarriage are now accepted or excused, not only as the norm for church members, but broadcast as proper for church leadership under the guise of "another chance." These teachings have not evolved through scriptural soundness nor historic precedence, but out of sociological expediency, compassionate compromise, and a distorted definition of "grace."

Be assured, there is a clear, concise, non-contradictive position in God's Word that is consistent with the earliest historic Christian New Testament teachings, written by holy, God-fearing men of the earliest centuries.

We must recognize this Trojan Horse for what it is, a heresy deceptively being infused into the Body of Christ.

Our Lord Jesus said to His followers: *"And ye shall know the truth, and the truth shall make you free."* John 8:32 Jesus prayed to the Father concerning His followers: *"Sanctify them through thy truth; thy word is truth."* John 17:17

God's people must declare what God's Word really says on this subject and expose the humanistic, rationalistic Erasmian View for what it is. If we fail to do this, the New Testament Church will be weakened and completely destroyed from within by this theological "Trojan Horse."

The New Testament Church must get back to a true New Testament doctrine of repentance, faith and holiness as revealed in God's Holy Word. We must demand the same of our Christian leaders as well as our schools of higher learning. Since the coming of our Lord Jesus is so near, it is crucial that this generation hear this message if the family structure, as we have historically known it, is to survive. If we fail here, it will affect us spiritually and nationally, for no nation or church body is any stronger than the individual families within it.

Historically, any nation or people who failed to maintain a biblical worldview concerning marriage has ceased to prosper spiritually.

Chapter 7

Clarifying Other Doctrinal Truths
❧❧

During seminar and conference teaching sessions several recurring subjects arose during the questions and answer periods following the lessons. Perhaps a brief discussion on grace, repentance and compassion would be helpful to insert here at this juncture.

While we realize it would be impossible to cover any of these basic questions extensively in this abbreviated treatise, we will try to emphasize the importance of recognizing our only righteousness is founded in and through the completed sacrifice of our Lord Jesus Christ, when He took on Himself our sins and bestowed upon us His righteousness. This is why Paul the Apostle said:

> *...There is none that doeth good, no, not one. Romans 3:11*

> *For all have sinned and come short of the glory of God. Romans 3:23*

> *That if thou shalt confess with thy mouth the Lord Jesus, and shalt believe in thine heart that God hath raised him from the dead, thou shalt be saved. Romans 10:9*

Throughout the Bible, God declares moral principles. He desires us to follow and obey His word; not to gain our salvation, but so we might live a life of blessing and fruitfulness. If we fail to heed His standards, we automatically reap what we sow, we suffer the consequences of our decisions. Paul said:

> *Be not deceived; God is not mocked: for whatsoever a man soweth, that shall he also reap. For he that soweth to the flesh shall of the flesh reap corruption; but he that soweth to the Spirit shall of the Spirit reap life everlasting. Galatians 6:7,8*

The Lord teaches us these eternal principles of life so we might experience His abundance and fruitfulness.

Grace

There are several prevailing definitions of grace being postulated today in schools of varying doctrinal persuasions.

One such definition is; "God's riches at Christ's expense." Another is; "Grace is receiving what we don't deserve, in contrast to mercy, which is not getting what we do deserve."

Perhaps a clearer definition of grace would be the one given by Bill Gothard, in his Basic Youth Conflicts Conferences: "The power to know and to do God's will." To say it another way would be, when anyone truly experiences God's grace, that one is given the ability not to continue in habitual sin and walk away from it victoriously. This description says, grace can reveal the truth from God's Word concerning marriage and divorce and empower us to walk out this revelation. May we each allow the Holy Spirit to impart this message into our spirit as we share the following verses:

> *What shall we say then? Shall we continue in sin, that <u>GRACE</u> may abound? God forbid. How shall we, that are dead to sin, live any longer therein? Romans 6:1-2*

This verse clearly says when one receives Christ as Lord and Savior, it does not give us liberty to keep sinning, but the power to have victory over sin. Grace that brings salvation is the same grace that helps us to see and forsake ungodly behaviors.

> *For the GRACE OF GOD THAT BRINGETH*
> *SALVATION hath appeared to all men,*
> *Teaching us that, denying ungodliness and*
> *worldly lusts, we should live soberly,*
> *righteously, and godly, in this present*
> *world; Looking for that blessed hope, and*
> *the glorious appearing of the great God and*
> *our Saviour Jesus Christ; Who gave himself*
> *for us, that he might redeem us FROM all*
> *iniquity, and purify unto himself a peculiar*
> *people, zealous of good works. These things*
> *speak, and exhort, and rebuke with all*
> *authority. Let no man despise thee. Titus 2:*
> *11-15*

What does *"denying ungodliness"* mean? If godliness means being like God, then ungodliness means being unlike God.

God the Father referred to Israel as His *"wife"* in Jeremiah 3, and then told about how she (Israel) had repeatedly committed adulteries and whoredoms against Him. Israel's adulterous behavior resulted in God giving her a *"bill of divorcement."* (v 8) God told Israel that if she would only *"repent,"* He would take her back for *"I Am married to you."* (v 14)

God divorced Israel, but has not, is not, and will not ever seek another wife. He is waiting for the restoration of his wife to this day. Therefore, to *"deny ungodliness"* means that we must do the same with our marriage partner.

This teaching concerning the permanency of marriage is **Pure Grace.** The enemy has stolen the New Testament doctrine of grace from the Church, which has resulted in the destruction of families everywhere. It takes more grace to pray through marriage difficulties than to renounce our vow to God, and destroy the symbol of Christ's relationship to His Church.

Repentance

Repentance is one of the most misunderstood words in the Church today. Some Christians say we no longer need to repent. They believe that God will totally forgive and wipe away sin as though it never happened without an act of repentance by the sinner. This erroneous teaching infers Paul was deluded when he taught the believers in Ephesus the need for repentance.

And how I kept back nothing that was profitable unto you, but have shewed you, and have taught you publicly, and from house to house. Testifying both to the Jews, and also to the Greeks, repentance toward God, and faith toward our Lord Jesus Christ. Acts 20:20,21

Repentance in its simplest form means to admit whatever sin or disobedience the Holy Spirit exposes in our life, and quit it! We quit it only when we turn 180 degrees from the disobedience and forsake it. It does not infer perfection, but progressively going in a new direction; to agree with God concerning our sin or disobedience and trust His grace to help us be overcomers and experience His promised blessings.

Compassion

The secular worldview permeating our churches today will only be altered when God's servants lose their fear of public opinion 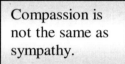 and realize they are Jesus Christ's representative to the world, declaring without fear or favor the clear teachings concerning the permanency of the marriage covenant which is the Biblical worldview.

If we desire to see the elimination of the bad fruit being produced in our society and our churches, we will need to replace the present day worldview with the true, historic biblical worldview concerning marriage, and cry out to God for the healing of our land.

If we are willing, God will do the same for us today, as He promised His people in Isaiah.

And therefore will the Lord wait, that he may be gracious unto you, and therefore will he be exalted, that he may have mercy upon you:

*for the Lord is a God of judgment: blessed
are all they that wait for him. For the people
shall dwell in Zion at Jerusalem: thou shalt
weep no more: he will be very gracious unto
thee at the voice of thy cry; when he shall
hear it, he will answer thee. Isaiah 30:18-19*

He promised mercy, forgiveness, and blessing
on Israel if they would just repent. I realize the true
repentance God wants us to experience will require
an adjustment of one's personal belief system. Our
decisions are based upon our belief system. And our
belief system should be based upon God's Word.

God's desire is for each of us to admit our non
biblical worldviews and forsake them so He can
show mercy.

*He that covereth his sin shall not prosper,
but who so confesseth and forsaketh them
shall have mercy. Proverbs 28:13*

In Corinthians, Paul said,
*For if we would judge ourselves, we should
not be judged. But when we are judged, we
are chastened of the Lord, that we should
not be condemned with the world.
I Corinthians 11:31-32*

As a child of God we are called to honor Jesus
Christ in every area of our lives. This is only possible
by drawing upon His Word, yielding to the Holy

Spirit, who will enable us to keep His commands and love the Lord with all our hearts, soul, mind and strength, and realize we are obligated to respond affirmatively when new principles for living are revealed to us by the Holy Spirit.

> John the Beloved wrote in II John,
> *Whosoever transgresseth and abideth not in the doctrine of Christ, hath not God. He that abideth in the doctrine of Christ, he hath both the Father and the Son. II John 9*

One of the surest evidences of being a believer in Christ is to see that believer willingly, knowingly, persistently obey the truth presented to him/her by the Holy Spirit. The writer of Hebrews says we will be sentenced when we fail to respond to Gods prompting. In fact we are warned;

> *to...despise* (to think down upon or feel it is of little significance) *not thou the chastening of the Lord, nor faint when thou art rebuked of him; for whom the Lord loveth he chasteneth, and scourgeth every son whom he receiveth. If ye endure chastening* (instruction) *God dealeth with you as with sons: for what son is he whom the father chasteneth not? But if ye be without chastisement, whereof all are partakers, then are ye bastards, and not sons. Hebrews 12:5-8*

The Lord loves His own and patiently instructs, forgives, encourages, and multiplies opportunities for his children to obey. Then He allows trials and tests to come to get our attention.

If we are violating God's will and word, but are not experiencing any correction or chastening, we need to immediately repent toward God, and place our faith in the finished work of Jesus Christ.

If we make Him Supreme Lord of our lives, we will obey and appreciate His loving, compassionate chastening. His loving kindness toward His own is from everlasting to everlasting toward them that fear Him.

This biblical worldview concerning marriage and divorce is difficult and must be taught with compassion; but what is biblical compassion? It is vitally important we understand the true biblical meaning of the word compassion. Compassion is not the same as sympathy. We can sympathize with the individual and their circumstances but we must stand firm on Biblical principles.

Note God's dealings with King Zedekiah. God defines compassion in II Chronicles 36. Zedekiah did evil in the Lord's sight and wouldn't humble himself before Nebuchadnezzar or Jeremiah the prophet. Verse 15 says God had *"compassion"* on His people and His temple. How did God have compassion on Israel?

> *"And the LORD God of their fathers sent to them by his messengers, rising up betimes,*

and sending; <u>because</u> <u>he</u> <u>had</u> <u>compassion</u>
<u>on</u> <u>his</u> <u>people,</u> and on his dwelling place."
II Chronicles 36:15

He showed His compassion by instructing them. Their response in verse 16 says, Israel *"mocked [God's] messengers."* What was the result? God sent the Chaldeans against them showing no compassion on them. (He chastened them.)

In the New Testament we read of how Jesus manifested divine compassion toward those following Him.

And Jesus, when he came out, saw much people, and was moved with compassion toward them, because they were as sheep not having a shepherd and he began to teach them many things. Mark 6:34

Whenever we teach anyone what God says, we manifest God's compassion. What the listeners do with the warning is their responsibility.

God is calling out and desires to speak to His people concerning the suffering due to divorce and remarriage today! He is trying to instruct us. Who will respond?

Chapter 8

Where Do We Go From Here?
꙯

Before we can ask, where do we go from here, we must determine where we are right now. In the light of the information we have just studied, and the realization of the incredible social, emotional, financial, and spiritual devastation it has produced, we must determine if we are prepared to make a life changing, quality decision, concerning what the Bible really says about marriage, divorce and remarriage.

If you are a pastor, we can identify with the consternation you are feeling because everything we were ever taught in the majority of commentaries we own justifies divorce and remarriage because they were written since the reformation. This is the only thing we have ever known. Few in leadership

today have ever been presented with the historic
evidence of the doctrinal change which took place
in the sixteenth century. We now know these same
reformers/writers of commentaries, were the ones
who changed the doctrine. We would urge you to
carefully reassess everything you have ever learned
in your years of training and your study about
divorce and remarriage. The greatest struggle we
encountered was being willing to reassess, by
proper hermeneutic principles and re-evaluating all
of our former convictions, regardless of the
outcome.

Remember how the Jewish leaders answered
Jesus when He asked them about John the Baptist's
ministry?

*And it came to pass, that on one of those
days, as he taught the people in the temple,
and preached the gospel, the chief priests
and the scribes came upon him with the
elders, and spake unto him, saying, Tell us,
by what authority doest thou these things?
Or who is he that gave thee this authority?
And he answered and said unto them, I will
also ask you one thing; and answer me: The
baptism of John, was it from heaven, or of
men? And they reasoned with themselves,
saying, If we shall say, From heaven; he will
say, Why then believed ye him not? But and
if we say, Of men; all the people will stone
us: for they be persuaded that John was a*

*prophet. And they answered, that they could
not tell whence it was. And Jesus said unto
them, Neither tell I you by what authority I
do these things. Luke 20:1-8*

Their answer had nothing to do with truth; but
situational realities: "if we say this, this will
happen; and if we say that, that will happen."
Consequently, they went away continuing to walk
in darkness. The bottom line for us should be two
things: what is my sole authority for all spiritual
decisions and whose bondservant am I? Paul the
Apostle declared all believers to be bond slaves of
Jesus Christ, whose responsibility is to be faithful to
Him. For every believer there is no other valid basis
for making a decision, but *"thus saith the Lord."*

Consider this; knowing we
are called to teach a very self
centered, self gratifying society,
is your teaching about marriage
and divorce and remarriage

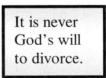

It is never
God's will
to divorce.

exactly like Jesus' and the apostle Paul's; or similar
to Erasmus' or the Reformers? You and I are by
products of what we have been taught or read
during our lifetime. It is virtually impossible to find
books teaching the New Testament position on
marriage and divorce in Christian bookstores today.
If we are to find the truth, we will have to do our
own research and be willing to face the firestorm in
our churches and denominational fellowships. Those

who have initiated a divorce and then remarried: have violated (not broken) many promises to love, honor and cherish their covenant partner and to cleave to them and them only, so long as they both should live, as stated in their marriage covenant; lied to their partner and to God, because they made a holy vow before God and many witnesses, "till death do us part." Thus by their abandoning of these promises, they are presently in a state of rebellion. Solomon said, in Proverbs 6:32 & *33; "But whoso committeth adultery with a woman lacketh understanding: he that doeth it destroyeth his own soul. A wound and dishonor shall he get; and his reproach (shame) shall not be wiped away."* (Young's Analytical Concordance to the Bible, says *"shall not be blotted out."*) No matter what they do, they cannot get away from the guilt and shame of their adulterous condition. This shame is in their spirit and remains. If we try to diminish this shame with man's reasoning or by ignoring Scripture, we will surely answer to God.

If what you have read has challenged you to seek further truth, may we suggest in the mean-time you might begin by refusing to marry another divorced person until you have this very serious issue completely settled in your own heart.

May we also suggest you never tell a couple who have been cohabiting, unmarried, they need to get married. Two wrongs do not make a right. They should first of all repent of their fornication and individually seek God's perfect will for their lives.

Only then should they evaluate if they truly love each other enough and have sufficiently common goals and convictions in life to consider becoming married. Until they have done this, they should not enter into the marriage covenant. That sin of fornication will then be under the blood. We know today the divorce rate of those who cohabit before marrying is much higher than those who marry and then live together.

If you are a single person; you can settle this issue in your heart once and for all, thus allowing you to make a clear choice in considering who will qualify as a future mate. Court the person you feel the Lord has shown you should be your future life partner. Refuse to "date." The same Holy Spirit that brought Joseph and Mary together can lead you to the perfect mate if you will wait on Him. Until then, keep yourself pure! If you will honor Him, He will honor you, in His perfect timing.

If He has called you to a life of celibacy, He will give you a peace about it and the grace to live a happy and fruitful life.

If you are presently seriously involved with another person, you can start now by keeping yourself pure. If you allow yourselves to be alone too much, the enemy can tempt you and try to destroy your testimony through lust. Become involved together in ministry outreach opportunities and studies to better prepare you for

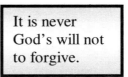

It is never God's will not to forgive.

future service together.

If you are already married, you can start by eliminating the "D" word from your vocabulary. Divorce must never be an option. God has called us to reconciliation and peace. Learn biblical principles concerning marriage and strive to encourage your partner in every way possible to be all they can be for His kingdom. Always be ready to forgive, encourage and edify your partner. Remember, the Lord made you "One flesh" but you and your partner must work at being of one heart, mind, and spirit, till death.

If you are already experiencing marital difficulties, we encourage you to re-focus your commitment to the Lordship of Jesus Christ. He promised to never leave you or forsake you. He invites us to (cast all our cares on Him because He cares for you.) He is looking for those who will follow Him regardless of our circumstances.

And there went great multitudes with him: and he turned, and said unto them, If any man come to me and hate not his father, and mother, and wife, and children, and brethren, and sister, yea and his own life also, he cannot be my disciple. And whosoever doth not bear his cross, and come after me, cannot be my disciple. For which of you, intending to build a tower, sitteth not down first, and counteth the cost, whether he have sufficient to finish it? Lest haply, after he hath laid the foundation, and is not able to finish it, all that behold it begin to mock him. Saying, This man began to build, and was not able to finish. Or what king, going to make war against another king, sitteth not down first, and consulteth whether he be able with ten thousand to meet him that cometh against him with twenty thousand? Or else, while the other is yet a great way off, he sendeth an ambassage, and desireth conditions of peace. So likewise, whosoever he be of you that forsaketh not all that he hath, he cannot be my disciple. Salt is good: but if the salt have lost his savour, wherewith shall it be seasoned? It is neither fit for the land, nor yet for the dunghill; but men cast it out. He that hath ears to hear, let him hear. Luke 14:25-35

Your present situation has not taken God by surprise and He is not finished with you. If you now realize you were at fault, confess it to God and your partner and ask the Lord to help you be more

> It is never God's will to violate a covenant.

like Jesus Christ in all your relationships, so your partner and others can see you are not who you once were.

Get busy serving the Lord in whatever way you can. Whatever you do, keep busy serving Him and other people in any way you can. Do not sit and soak! Do not go to a church where they encourage you to go to the "singles group" and pick out another partner. Do not listen to others who tell you to "forget your former mate and go on with your life." That counsel is not scriptural, and invites disaster into your life. Acknowledge the fact you and your partner are one flesh until death and only then, will the covenant cease.

Your partner may have already remarried but that act is only on their account. It will not be on your account until you respond in an ungodly way. Keep your record clean and continue to love, pray for, and encourage your life partner.

If you are parents of a young couple who are unhappily married, do not encourage them in any way to divorce, regardless how perfect your child has been in the whole situation. Even if you despise your child's partner, never encourage them to violate the covenant, but to find God's answer.

Let me be clear about one thing. We <u>have</u> encouraged some couples to separate where there has been mental, emotional, and/or physical abuse.

And unto the married, I command, yet not I, but the Lord, Let not the wife depart from her husband: But and if she depart, let her remain unmarried, or be reconciled to her husband: and let not the husband put away his wife. I Corinthians 7:10-11

In each of these instances, we have made it very clear to them they are still married and must not go looking for another partner. They should spend this time praying and studying to see how they might restore their relationship in a way pleasing to the Lord. We could give you many such illustrations of those who waited; and how the Lord did restore and bring healing.

The only place to go on from here, is into a more intimate relationship with The Lord Jesus Christ, putting Him, His word, and His will first place in your life. Only then will the *"peace of God which passes all understanding, keep your hearts and minds through Christ Jesus." Philippians 4:7*

First, we must tell you emphatically that God loves you more than you can ever know in your mind. Remember, He sent His Son, Jesus, to be the final solution for our sin and separation from God. At a time like this, it is important to remember it was our Lord Jesus who warned us to count the cost before we committed our lives to Him. Luke 14:25-35 says He demands our unrivaled love and obedience or we *"cannot be His disciples."*

Grace is a powerful tool in God's hands to help us overcome every difficult situation and He promises He will never put more on us than we can bear. Grace does not hide or skirt around the problem, but rather confronts it until it is completely resolved. Therefore, since you are under God's grace, you have the power to overcome what seems to be an impossible situation.

To repent of any sin is to turn away from it and go in the other direction. To repent of a sin means to stop doing it. In other words, the only way a thief stops being a thief is if he/she quits stealing. Likewise, the only way to stop being an adulterer/adulteress, is to stop committing adultery.

God is so faithful! If you will seek His face, He will help you to be faithful as well. Faithful obedience to His word in every situation is the clarion call of the Gospel of Jesus Christ. Remember, breaking the cycle of any sin may seem impossible at first, but by His grace, you have the power within you to do it. Sin, not repented of, passes from generation to generation, and only you, by genuine biblical repentance can stop the cycle now.

When you're ready, pray this prayer and begin to take hold of God's promise to lead you to total obedience and victory in your present situation:

Heavenly Father. The Holy Spirit has revealed truth to me I never understood before. The weight of my disobedience, though in ignorance, leaves me feeling like I'm being crushed under this burden of past failures and sin. I didn't realize how wrong my choices were; but now, the fruit of them has led me to this difficult place in my life. I pray that You will forgive me and completely deliver me from these sins.

I am trusting You, Lord, to help me walk through this, experiencing your love and peace in the midst of this storm. Help me to be the person You have called me to be and to respond to your Spirit's convicting influence in my life, by appropriating Your love and compassion.

Lord, I thank You for this truth. I resolve before You to do what is necessary to bring my life and the lives of my loved ones into agreement with Your truth. Thank you for hearing me. In Jesus' Name I pray. Amen.

Please remember; God's love is unconditional toward His children and He is waiting to see what you and I will do with His truth. Paul Said, in Galatians 6:8:

> *"For he that soweth to his flesh shall of his flesh reap corruption; but he that soweth to the Spirit, shall of the Spirit reap life ever-lasting."* AMEN!

Now that we understand the difference between New Testament truth and rationalistic/humanistic reasoning of men; it is imperative that we ask ourselves: Whom shall we then believe?

Chapter 9

Conclusion
❧❧

If you're called to preach the whole counsel of God, and you preach the Word of God uncompromisingly, God will honor you!

The resistance against this biblical truth has become extremely strong. So strong, in fact, that many believers who say they believe marriage is for life and only death breaks the marriage covenant, are being ridiculed and persecuted.

Pastors and Christian leaders, we challenge you to remember, the work of God's watchmen is not to delight, pacify, or titillate those under your care. Your task is to let His Word reverberate like a trumpet, a clear, articulate alarm whenever the enemy appears. The trumpet call must not infer uncertainty or doubt, but rouse the city to definite action. If the watchman fails here, the blood of the city will be on his hands and the shame of his failure will never leave him.

Oh watchman, sound the warning. The **Trojan Horse** is already in the city.

Son of man, I have made thee a watchman... therefore hear the word at my mouth, and give them warning from Me. *Ezekiel 3:17*

Isaiah said;
Also I heard the voice of the Lord, saying, whom shall I send, and who will go for us? Then said I, Here am I, send me. Isaiah 6:8

The Lord seeks leaders who fear Him more than men, denominations, traditional thinking, or financial security. God desires leaders who treasure His approval more than the approval of men; those who are willing to forsake everything, to be His disciple.

We refer again to Francis Schaeffer, who wrote a book in 1976 entitled, *How Shall We Then Live?* Schaeffer laid out two worldviews, the secular and the biblical, and contrasted them, declaring we must all decide how we will live in the light of these two worldviews.

As we stated in the introduction, today, we are faced with a similar dilemma. We are confronted with a secular (humanistic) worldview which Joel Belz, Founder of the well known World Christian news magazine; calls "nominalism, and you might well conclude as being practical secularism." If we are to hold to a biblical worldview concerning divorce and remarriage, the question must still be answered; Whom shall we then believe? Should we believe Jesus, Paul, and the earliest Church Fathers or should we believe Erasmus and the Reformers? It was Paul who commanded Timothy, *"Follow me even as I also am of Christ," I Corinthians 12:1.* This critical question must be answered because of the devastating consequences the present day teaching has brought upon the Christian community.

Paul received his message directly from Jesus Christ and passed it on to Timothy so he could pass it on to *"faithful men." II Timothy 2:2*

The position of the earliest Church Fathers and the position of Erasmus and the reformers are in total opposition to each other, so both cannot be right.

Whom shall we then believe? That question must be answered by each of us individually.

Every verse of Scripture relating to marriage and divorce when properly exegeted, comes into total harmony historically, hermeneutically, exegetically and doctrinally. It is imperative for us to see how far the Church has strayed in its present day teachings from God's eternal purpose for marriage. Study it with your Bible open. Get its truth down into your heart and lovingly warn others before it is too late.

We must remember:
"The fear of the Lord is the beginning of wisdom..." Palm 111:10 and, *"The fear of man bringeth a snare." Proverbs 29:2*

Scriptural Index
❧❧

Romans	10:9	120
	12:10	55
I Corinthians	6:9-11	50
	6:10	110
	7:3-5a	50
	7:10-11	2, 96, 99, 136
	7:15	49
	11:31-32	125
	12:1	143
II Corinthians	1:23	114
Galatians	1:11,12	2
	1:20	114
	5:19	110
	6:7,8	120, 139
Philippians	4:7	137
I Timothy	4:1	56
II Timothy	2:1,2	1
	2:2	33, 143
	4:2-4a	57
Hebrews	11:32	107
	12:5-8	126
	12:16-17	99
James	5:12	114
II John	9	126

Index of Historic Persons
~⊱⊰~

Bibliography

❧❧

Allen, P.S. *"The Age Of Erasmus."* Clarendon Press. Oxford University, 1914.

Augustijn, Cornelius. *"Erasmus, His Life, Works and Influence."* Translated by J. C. Grayson. University of Toronto Press, 1991.

Bainton, Roland H. *"Erasmus of Christendom."* Charles Scribner's Sons. New York. 1969.

Dickens, A.G. *"The Age of Humanism and Reformation: Europe in The Fourteenth, Fifteenth and Sixteenth Century."* Prentice Hall Inc. Englewood Cliffs, NJ.

Hertz, J. H. ed. *"The Pentateuch and Haftorah."* [2nd] Ed. Sancino Press. London. 1988.

Heth, William A and Wenham, Gordon J. *"Jesus And Divorce: The Problem With The Evangelical Consensus."* Thomas Nelson Publishers. Nashville, Camden, New York 1985.

Koenigsberger, H. G, Mosse, George L. and Bowler, G.Q. *"Europe in the Sixteenth Century."* [2nd] Ed. Longman. London and New York.

Murphy, Anne. *Thomas More.* "Great Christian Thinkers Series." Edited by Peter Vardy. Triumph Press. Liguori, Missouri.

Newcombe, D.G. *"Henry VIII and the English Reformation."* Routledge. London, New York. 1995.

Olsen, Viggo Norskov. *"The New Testament Logia on Divorce.A Study of their Interpretation from Erasmus to Milton."* J.C B. Mohr (Paul Sibeck). Tubingen. 1971

Pettegree, Andrew. *"Europe In The Sixteenth Century."* Blackwell Publishers.

Roth, Allen. "Do Divorced and Remarried Persons Need to Separate?: An Act or a State?" Article.

Sanders, E.P. *"Jesus and Judaism."* Fortress Press. Philadelphia

Smith, Preserved. *"Erasmus A Study of His Life, Ideals and Place in* History." Dover Publications, Inc. New York. 1962

Thompson, S. Harrison. *"Europe in Renaissance and Reformation."* Harcourt, Brace & world, Inc. New York, Burlingame.

Zwieg, Stefan. *"Erasmus of Rotterdam."* Translated by Eden and Cedar Paul. Garden City Publishing Co. Garden City, New York, 1937.

_____, "Erasmus 1469-1536." Internet web site. http://www.hfac.uh.edu/gbrown/philosophers/leibniz/ BritannicaPages/Erasmus/Erasmus.html.

_____, "English Bible History: John Colet" Internet web site. http://greatsite.com/timeline-english-bible-history/ john-colet.html.

_____, "Erasmus." Internet web site. http://en.wikipedia. org/wiki/Erasmus

_____,"Erasmus, Desiderius" Internet Web site.

Resources Available
❧❧

Till Death Do Us Part

What is the marriage law? When was the marriage law established? To whom does the marriage law apply: What constitutes a biblical marriage: Does the New Testament ever recognize divorce? What about the biblical exceptions? What is the biblical procedure for knowing my past is forgiven?

Scriptural Standards for a Pastor

These tapes contain an in depth study of the biblical requirements for one called to be a pastor. Many pastors will never teach on this subject because of fear or embarrassment, but the word of God is very clear and must be understood by believers who are looking for a Biblically qualified pastor.

Peacekeeper or Peacemaker, Which Are You?

God has used this tape to radically change the lives of thousands. Already, this teaching strips away all the excuses for compromise and makes clear the purpose of calling God's people to be salt or light.

Biblical Principles of Christian Living

Here is a clear and comprehensive study of perti-

nent biblical principles regarding courting, engagement, marriage, starting a family, rearing a family,
inter-personal relationships within a family, parenting
and grandparenting.

**To see these and other helpful resources please
visit our website at www.cpr-ministries.org.**

Christian Principles Restored Ministries International, Inc. is an interdenominational, religious non-profit corporation and a faith ministry, supported solely through gifts and offerings of faithful Christians. Its purpose for existence is to reestablish true Biblical principles in the Church concerning courting, engagement, marriage and divorce, and to promote Christ-centered homes and families. We would love to hear from you.

CPR Ministries International Inc.
P.O. Box 520729
Longwood, FL 32752-0729

Phone 407.834.5233

info@cpr-ministries.org
www.cpr-ministries.org

End Notes

[i] Theological Foundations Ministries. All rights reserved, Rev. Stephen W. Wilcox © 2004. Used by permission.

[ii] Compiled and categorized by the <u>Christian Classics Ethereal Classics Library.</u> All ancient material quoted is in the public domain and may be copied freely. The forgoing material is edited from <u>www.marriagedivorce.com,</u> a home page of Theological Foundations Ministries. All rights reserved, Rev. Stephen W. Wilcox © 2004 Used by permission.

[iii] Author's note: Latest research indicates that Ambrosiaster may have been a fictitious name.

[iv] Steele, Paul E. and Ryrie, Charles C., <u>Meant To Last</u> (Wheaton, IL: Victor Books, 1983), 1983, pp. 88-89, (out of print).

[v] Smith, Preserved, Erasmus, <u>A Study of His Life, Ideals, and Place in History,</u> (New York: Frederick Unger Publishing Co., 1962), pp. 14, 27,29,60,367.

[vi] Erasmus, Desiderius, Microsoft Encarta Online

Encyclopedia 2005 http://encarta.msn.com 1997-2005 Microsoft Corporation. All rights Reserved.

vii *Erasmus: His Life, Works and Influence* by Cornelius Augustin & J.C. Grayson; University of Toronto Press, 1991

viii *Erasmus of Christendom* by Roland H. Bainton, New York; Charles Scribner's Sons Copyright 1969

ix *"The N.T. Logia on Divorce: A Study of Their Interpretation, from Erasmus to Milton."* By V.N. Olsen; J.C.B. Mohr. (Paul Siebeck) 1971 p. 15

x *Erasmus A Study of His Life, Ideals and Place in History* by Preserved Smith, Ph. D., Litt.D., Dover Publications Inc., N.Y. 1962 p. 429

xi *The N.T. Logia on Divorce: A Study of Their Interpretation, from Erasmus to Milton"* by V.N. Olsen; J.C.B. Mohr (Paul Siebeck) 1971 p. 23

xii *Erasmus of Christendom* by Roland Bainter, New York; Charles Scribner's Sons 1969 pp. 229-231

xiii *"The N.T. Logia on Divorce: A Study of Their Interpretation, from Erasmus to Milton"* by V.N. Olsen; J.C.B. Mohr (Paul Siebeck) 1971 p.26

xiv *Erasmus of Christendom* by Roland Bainter, New York; Charles Scribner's Sons 1969 pp. 229-231

xv *Jesus and Divorce: The Problem With The Evangelical Consensus* by William A Heth and Gordon J. Wenham: by Thomas Nelson Publishers; Nashville, Camden, New York p. 75,76

xvi   "The N.T. Logia on Divorce: A Study of Their Interpretation, from Erasmus to Milton" by V.N. Olsen; J.C.B. Mohr (Paul Siebeck) 1971 p.22

xvii   "The N.T. Logia on Divorce: A Study of Their Interpretation, from Erasmus to Milton" by V.N. Olsen; J.C.B. Mohr (Paul Siebeck) 1971 p.46

xviii Ibid

xix   Ibid

xxii   "The N.T. Logia on Divorce: A Study of Their Interpretation, from Erasmus to Milton" by V.N. Olsen; J.C.B. Mohr (Paul Siebeck) 1971

xxiii Erasmus of Christendom by Roland Bainter, New York; Charles Scirbner's Sons. 1969 pp.229-231

xxiv   Ibid

xxv   Hermeneutics by Professor D. R. Dungan; Standard Publishing Company. Used by permission.)

xxvi   Till Death Do Us Part? Dr. Joseph A. Webb

xxvii 3/17/07 World Magazine, "Standing in the God Gate." p. 6